Daidōji Yuzān's

Code of the Samurai

A Contemporary Dual-Language Edition
of the Bushidō Shoshinshū

Daidōji Yuzān's

Code of the Samurai

Translated by **A. L. Sadler**   Illustrated by **Miro Salazar**

Ulysses Press

Published by:
Ulysses Press
P.O. Box 3440
Berkeley, CA 94703
www.ulyssespress.com

ISBN10: 1-56975-590-6
ISBN13: 978-1-56975-590-7
Library of Congress Control Number 2006938954

Printed in the United States by Bang Printing

10 9 8 7 6 5 4 3 2 1

Acquisitions Editor: Nick Denton-Brown
Managing Editor: Claire Chun
Editor: Mark Woodworth
Consulting Editor: Jon Babcock
Editorial Associate: Elyce Petker
Cover design: Double R Design
Interior design and layout: what!design @ whatweb.com

Distributed by Publishers Group West

Contents

Translator's Note

The historical documents that illustrate the main concepts connected with Bushido,* or Japanese chivalry are, in earlier days,
the various accounts of the activities of the warrior in war and
peace, and later on the House Laws and sets of maxims drawn
up by the great feudal lords or sometimes by lesser personages.
Among the latter is this textbook for young samurai which
purports to lay down what was required of them in the latter
half of the seventeenth and early eighteenth century. The author
was an expert in the military arts and a prominent writer of
those days, and since he lived to the age of 92 under the rule
of six shoguns from Iemitsu to Yoshimune—he was 12 when
Iemitsu died and Yoshimune had been shogun for 15 years
when he himself died—he had known the atmosphere of the
early Tokugawa period as it was only a decade after the death
of Ieyasu, and had lived to see the splendor of the Genroku age
under the luxurious and eccentric Tsunayoshi. As a retainer
[or servant] of the Tokugawa house he was familiar with the
work and teachings of the sage Mitsukuni, Lord of Mito, and
was also the pupil of Yamaga Sokō, another eminent writer on
Bushido and seventeen years his senior. He had witnessed the
heroic example of the Forty-Seven Loyal Rōnin of Akō, whose
leader Ōishi Yoshio was another pupil of Sokō, and also the ruin
of more than one feudal lord owing to domestic trouble caused
by the machinations of evil retainers. He was the contemporary
also of the great scholar Arai Hakuseki, whose well-known
autobiography gives a picture of a samurai family very much

according to his ideal. Few can have been better qualified to expatiate on this subject, and his advice as to what the samurai should avoid is very clearly based on the falling away from the austerity and simplicity of the "days of old" that he had in his later days experienced and which the Shogun Yoshimune with his principle of "back to Ieyasu" tried so earnestly to correct. And his work gives a very clear and lively account of Bushido as he knew it, perhaps more succinct than can be found elsewhere, while more detailed than such sets of articles as the "Hundred Rules" of Takeda Shingen or of Ieyasu. Moreover, it is written entirely from the point of view of the retainer and not of the lord. For this reason I have used the word "samurai" in it instead of "bushi," which is not so familiar to readers of English, though it is more comprehensive as meaning the military man or warrior and therefore including the daimyo, or feudal lord, which the term samurai does not. "Samurai" is an expression of respectable antiquity incidentally, and a pure Japanese one, first used in the sense of military retainer in the tenth century, and adopted in the late twelfth century by the Kamakura military government as the official designation of the War Department or Samurai-dokoro.

Daidōji Yūzan Shigesuke was of a distinguished samurai family claiming descent from the Taira clan through Taira Korehira (10th century). His ancestor in the fifth generation was Shigetoki, elder brother of Ise Shinkurō Nagauji, who became famous as Hōjō Sōun, lord of Odawara, and one of the outstanding warrior administrators of his day. Shigetoki took the name of Daidōji from the village where he retired. His grandson Masashige committed suicide when Odawara was taken by Hideyoshi in 1590, and his son Naoshige became a vassal of Tokugawa Hidetada and fought valiantly at the siege of Osaka, helping to rally the Shogun's troops when they were badly shaken by the desperate charge of the garrison. Yūzan's father, Shigehisa, was a vassal of Tokugawa Tadateru, Ieyasu's sixth son and younger brother of Hidetada, who became suspect, lost his fief, and was retired. Yūzan seems to have followed his father as his retainer for a time, but meanwhile he studied and became an orthodox Confucian scholar and expert in military affairs and took a position as military adviser to Lord Matsudaira of Aizu. He then retired to Iwabuchi in Musashi, but later on went to live in the household of Matsudaira, Echizen no Kami, chief of the Kamon or direct relative houses of the Shogun. Evidently he practiced what he recommended, for he is described as a pattern of loyalty, self-control, and equanimity. He was also a verse writer of some note. As an author he is well known for the *Iwabuchi Yawa,* or "Evening Chats at Iwabuchi," a series of anecdotes about Tokugawa Ieyasu arranged in chronological order, and the perhaps more familiar *Ochiboshu,* a history of Ieyasu and his connections and successors, and of the city and castle of Edo which they built. He also wrote the *Taishōden,* or "Records of Great Commanders," and the *Goshinron,* or "Essays on Five Vassals."

---

*The word "Bushido," like "Samurai," has become a loan word in English and is explained as "The national spirit of Japan, especially the military spirit, traditional chivalry as of the old Samurai class." Its literal meaning is "the Way of the Warrior" and it is found in Japanese first in the late sixteenth century, e.g. in the legacy of Torii Mototada (1539–1600), and elsewhere. Some European writers, following Chamberlain, have maintained that both the word and what it signifies are inventions of the Meiji period [1868–1912] intended to fortify national sentiment and unknown before. The currency of the word in the West is no doubt chiefly due to the book called *Bushido* published in 1899 by Dr. Nitobe, whence the careless statement in a largely circulated popular American work on the thought of the Orient, "Bushido, a word invented by Inazo Nitobe."

Code of the Samurai
武道初心集

總論

武士たらむものは。正月元日の朝。雑煮の餅を祝ふとて。箸を取初るより。其年の大晦日の夕べに至るまで。日々夜々死を常に心にあつるを以て。本意の第一と仕り候。死をさへ常に心にあて候へば。忠孝の二つの道にも相叶ひ。萬の惡事災難をも遁れ。其身無病息災にして。壽命長久に。剩へ其人柄までもよろしく罷成。其徳おほき事に候。

Introduction

He who is a samurai must before all things keep always in mind, by day and by night, from the morning when he takes up his chopsticks to eat his New Year's breakfast to Old Year's night when he pays his yearly bills, the fact that he has to die. That is his chief business. If he is always mindful of this, he will be able to live in accordance with the paths of Loyalty and Filial Duty, will avoid myriads of evils and adversities, will keep himself free from disease and calamity, and will enjoy a long life. He will also be a fine personality with many admirable qualities.

其仔細を申に。總じて人間の命をば。夕部の露。あしたの霜になぞ
らへ。隨分はかなき物に致し置候中にも。殊更危きは武士の身命
にて候を。人々おのれが心ずましに。いつまでも長生を仕る了簡な
るに依て。主君へも末永き御奉公。親々への孝養も。末久しき義
なりと存ずるから事起りて。主君へも不奉公を仕り。親々への孝
行も。疎略には罷成にて候。今日在て明日を知らぬ身命とさへ。覺
悟仕り候に於ては。主君の御前へ罷出て御用を承るも。親々の顔
を見上るも。是をかぎりと罷成事もやと。存ずる心あひに相成候ゆ
ゑ。主親へ眞實の思ひ入れと罷成らずしてはかなはず候。去に依
て。忠孝の二つの道にも相叶ふとは申にて候。

拠又死を忘れて油斷致す心より。物に愼しみなく。人の氣に障る事
をも云て口論に及び。聞捨に仕りて事濟儀をも。聞咎めて物云に
仕なし。或は無益なる遊山見物の場所。人込の中といふ遠慮もな
く。ありきまはり。えしれぬ馬鹿者などにも出逢。不慮の喧嘩に及
び。身命を果して主君の御名を出し。親兄弟に難儀を懸る事。皆
常に死を心にあてぬ油斷より起る禍ひに候。死を常に心に當る時
は物をいふも。人の物云返答を致すも。武士の身にては。一言の甲
乙を大事と心得るを以て。譯もなき口論などを不仕。勿論むさと致
したる場所へは。人が誘ひても行ざるゆゑ。不慮の首尾に出合ふ
べき様も是なく候。爰を以て萬の惡事災難をも遁るゝとは申に
て候。

For existence is impermanent as the dew of evening and the hoarfrost of morning, and particularly uncertain is the life of the warrior. If he thinks he can console himself with the idea of eternal service to his lord or unending devotion to his relatives, something may well happen to make him neglect his duty to his lord and forget what he owes to his family. But if he determines simply to live for today and take no thought for the morrow, so that when he stands before his lord to receive his commands he thinks of it as his last appearance and when he looks on the faces of his relatives he feels that he will never see them again, then will his duty and regard for both of them be completely sincere, while his mind will be in accord with the paths of Loyalty and Filial Duty.

But if he does not keep death in mind, he will be careless and liable to be indiscreet and say things that offend others. Though nothing may come of it, if an argument ensues and he is rebuked, it may end in a quarrel. Then, if he goes strolling around pleasure resorts and seeing the sights in crowded places without proper restraint, he may come up against some big fool and get into a quarrel before he knows it, and may even be killed and his lord's name brought into it and his parents and relations exposed to disgrace. All this misfortune springs from his not remembering to keep death always in his thoughts. But one who does this, whether he is speaking himself or answering others, will carefully consider, as befits a samurai, every word he says and never launch into useless argument. Neither will he allow anyone to entice him into unsuitable places where he may be suddenly confronted with an awkward situation, and thus he avoids evils and calamities.

貴きも賤しきも。人は死を忘るゝゆゑに。常に過食大酒淫欲等の不養生を致し。脾腎の煩を仕出し。思ひの外なる若死をも致し。たとひ存命にても。何の用に立ざる病者とはなり果候。死を常に心にあつる時は。其身の年も若く。無病息災なりといへども。兼て補養の心得を致し。飲食を節に仕り。色の道をも遠ざけ。たしなみ愼しみ候故に。其身も壯健に候。扨こそ無病息災にて。壽命までも長久なりとは申にて候。

其上此世の逗留を永く存ずるに付。色々の望みも出來。欲心深くなり候て。人の物といへば欲しがり。我が物をば惜しみ。悉皆町人體の意地あひのごとくには罷成にて候。死を常に心にあつる時は。貪欲の心もおのづから薄くなり。ほしきをしきのむさき意地あひも。左のみさし出ざる道理に候。去に依て。其人柄までも宜しくなるとは申にて候。

但し死をいかに心に當ればとて。吉田の兼好がつれづれ草に書置たる。心戒と申比丘がごとく。二六時中死期を待心にて。いつもたゞうづくまりてのみ罷在候は。出家沙門の修行にはいかんも候へ。武道修行の本意には相叶ひ不申候。左様に死をあて候ては。主親へ忠孝の道も捨り。武士の家業も欠果申なれば。大きに宜しからず候。晝夜を限らず。公私の諸用を仕廻ひ。しばらくも身の暇ありて。心靜なる時は。死の一字を思ひ出し。懈怠なく心にあてよと申事にて候。楠正成が子息正行に申教へし言葉にも。常に死をならへと有之由承り傳へ候。初心の武士心得のため仍如件。

And samurai both high and low, if they forget about death, are apt to indulge in food and wine and women to unhealthy excess, so that they die unexpectedly early from diseases of the kidneys and spleen, and even while they live their illness makes them of no use to anyone. But those who keep death always before their eyes are strong and healthy while young, and when they take care of their health and are moderate in eating and drinking and avoid the paths of women, being restrained and moderate in all things, they remain free from disease and live a long and healthy life.

But one who lives long in this world may develop all sorts of desires, and his covetousness may increase so that he wants what belongs to others and cannot bear to part with what is his own, becoming in fact exactly like a shopkeeper. But if he is always staring death in the face, a man will have little attachment to material things and will not exhibit these grasping and greedy qualities. He will become, as I said before, a fine character.

And speaking of meditation on death, Yoshida Kenko says in the *Tsurezure-Gusa* of the monk Shinkai that he was inclined to sit all day long pondering on his last days; this is, no doubt, a very suitable attitude for a recluse but not for a warrior. For so he would have to neglect his military duties and the Way of Loyalty and Filial Piety, and he must on the contrary be constantly busy with his affairs, both public and private. But whenever he has some spare time to himself and can be quiet, he should not fail to return to this question of death and reflect carefully on it. Is it not written that Kusunoki Masashize commanded his son Masatsura to keep death always before his eyes? All this is for the instruction of the youthful samurai.

教育

武士たらむものは。三民の上に立て。事を執る職分の義に候へば。學問を致し。博く物の道理を辨へ不申しては不叶義に候。然りといへども亂世の武士と申は。生れて十五六歳にも罷成候得ば。必ず初陣に立て。一騎役をも相務め申なれば。十二三の年來より。武藝を修練致し候に付。見臺に向ひ書物を抜き。机にもたれて筆を把るべき身の暇とては。左のみ無之を以て。おのづから無學文盲にして。一文字を引ことさへならぬ様なる武士。戰國にはいかほども有之候。去れどもあながち其身の不心掛とも。親々の教への惡しきとも沙汰無之候は。武道を專一とかせぐを以て。當用と仕るが故にて候。

今天下靜謐の世に生れ値たる武士とても。武道の心懸を疎略に致して。苦しからずと申にては無之候へども。亂世の武士のごとく。十五六歳よりは。是非軍陣に不立しては。叶はずと申間にても無之候へば。七八歳の年齡にも生立候に於ては。四書五經七書等の文字讀をも致させ。手習をも仕りて。物を書覺え候様にと。油斷なく申教へ。扨十五六歳にも罷成候得ば。弓を射馬に乗り。其外一切の武藝をも修煉致させ候義。治世の武士。子を育つる本意たるべく候。右に申亂世の武士の文盲なるには。一通りの申わけも有之候。治世の武士の無筆文盲の申分けは。立兼申義に候。但し子供の義は咎むべきにも無之候。偏に親々の油斷不調法と可申にて候。畢竟子を愛する道を知らざるがゆえに候。初心の武士心得のため仍如件。

Education

Because the samurai stands at the head of the three classes of society and has the duty of carrying on the administration, he is obliged to become well educated and to gain a wide knowledge of the reason of things. In the period of civil war, however, the young warrior went out to battle when he was fifteen or sixteen, so he had to start his military education at twelve or thirteen. Since he had no time to sit down with a book or take up a writing brush, he was often totally illiterate. In fact, in those days there were many samurai who could not write a single Chinese character. So whether through their own lack of desire or the faulty instruction of their parents, nothing was done about it, because their whole life was devoted exclusively to the Way of the Warrior.

Now, though, the empire is at peace, and though one cannot exactly say that those born in samurai families are indifferent to military training, yet there is no question of their being forced to enter a warlike career at the age of fifteen or sixteen like the warrior of former days. So at the age of seven or eight, when he is growing up, a boy should be introduced to the Four Books, the Five Classics, and the Seven Texts and taught calligraphy so that he remembers how to write characters. Then, when he is fifteen or sixteen, he should practice archery and horsemanship and all the other military arts, for that is the way that the samurai should bring up his own sons in time of peace. There is no excuse for illiteracy in such a youth, unlike that of the warrior of the civil war period. And, in any case, children are not to blame for their lack of education, which is entirely due to the neglect and incompetence of their parents, who do not truly know the way of affection for their children.

孝行

武士たらむものは。親へ孝養のつとめの厚きを以て根本と仕り候。たとひ利發才覺人に勝れ。辯舌明らかにして。器量よろしく生れ付候ても。親へ不孝のものは。何の用にも立不申候。子細を申に。武士道は本末を正しく致すを以て。肝要と仕る事にて候。本末の辨へ無之候ては。義理を知るべき様無之候。義理を知らざるものは。武士とは申がたく候。本末を知ると申は。親は我身の本にして。我が身は親の骨肉の末と申義を辨へ候事に候。然るに其末たる我が身を立る心から事起りて。根本たる親をば疎略に仕るにて候。是本末を辨へざる故に候。

Filial Duty

He who is a samurai should base his conduct on a strong sense of his duty as befits a son. However capable and clever and eloquent and handsome one may be born, if he is unfilial he is of no use at all. Bushido, the Way of the Warrior, requires a man's conduct to be correct in every respect. For if there is no discrimination in all matters, there will be no knowledge of what is right. And one who does not know what is right can hardly be called a samurai. Now he who has this complete insight realizes that his parents are the authors of his being and that he is part of their flesh and blood. It is from the tendency to exalt this part which is ourselves that things sometimes happen that lead us to minimize our parental origin. This is want of truly understanding the order of cause and effect.

抵又親へ孝養を盡すに二段の様子有之候。たとへば其親の心だ
てすなほにして。慈愛の誠を以て教育に預り。其上人の取得がた
き高知行に。武具馬具家財に至るまで事欠なく。剩へ宜しき嫁ま
でとり迎へて。何に不足なき家督を讓り。おのれは隱居となりたる
親々へは。其子として常大體の孝養にては。譽所も感じ所も無之
候。赤の他人にても入魂のうへ。我身上勝手向の事までも。苦勞
に預り候ものへは。此方からも女才を致さず。たとひ手前の事をさ
し置ても。其人の用事ならばと思ふ様にも罷成候。況や我が親とし
て慈愛の心深く。其仕様仕方ともに。殘る所もなきに於ては。其子
の身にては。いか程孝養に力を盡し候とも。是にて事足れりと存ず
る義は無之筈に候。爰を以て只尋常の孝行にては。感じ所も無之
とは申にて候。

其親の心だて直ならず。其上老僻みてくだらぬ理窟立ばかりを申。
何一色我家督と有て。讓り與へたる品も無之。勝手不如意なる辨
へもなく。朝夕の飲物食物衣類等に付ても。種々のねだり事を申。
剩へ他所他門のものに出逢ては。倅めが不孝ゆゑ。老後に存寄ら
ぬ苦勞を仕り。思召の外迷惑致すなどゝ申觸れて。我が子の外聞
を失はせ候様なる。

Now, in rendering filial obligations to parents there are two varieties. The first is where the parent's disposition is honest and he educates his children with sincere kindliness and leaves them all his property. This may include giving them an income above the average, together with weapons and horse furniture and household treasures, as well as arranging good marriages for them. When such a parent retires it is neither praiseworthy nor remarkable that his children should look after him and treat him with all consideration. Even toward a complete outsider, if he is a bosom friend and goes out of his way to be helpful to us, we feel very kindly disposed and do anything we can for him, though it may be contrary to our own interests. How much deeper, then, must the bond of affection be where our parents are concerned? So, however much we do for them as children, we cannot help feeling that though we try hard to perform our filial duties it is never really enough. And this is simply the ordinary filial piety, nothing at all remarkable.

But if the parent is not kindly but old and cranky and is always nagging, he may insist that the household property belongs to him, may give his children nothing, and without considering the scarce resources of the family may constantly be making all kinds of urgent demands for drink and food and clothes. And not only that, but whenever he meets other people he says something like this: "This wretched son of mine is unfilial, and so I have to put up with all sorts of discomfort. You have no idea what a bad time I have in my old age," thus giving his children a bad name among outsiders.

分別相違の親をも親とあがまへ。取にくき機嫌をとり。偏に親の老
衰をかなしみ嘆きて。毛頭も女才を致さず。孝養の誠を盡すを。孝
子の本意とは申にて候。如此の意地ある武士は主君をとり奉公の
身となり候ても。忠義の道をも能わきまへ。主君の御威勢盛なる時
は申に及ばず。たとひ御身上に不慮の義出来。御難義千萬なる節
は。獪以て眞忠を勵まし。味方百騎が十騎になり。十騎が一騎に
なるまでも。御側を立はなれず。幾度も敵の矢おもてに立塞がりて。
身命をかへり見ぬ様なる軍忠をも勤め兼ず候。

親と主と。孝と忠といふ名のかはる迄にて。心の誠に二つは無之
候。去るに依て古人の詞にも。忠臣をば孝子の門に求めよと有之
由に候。たとひ親へこそ不孝に候共。主君へ忠貞は格別なりと申
義は。決して無之道理に候。己が身の根本たる親へさへ。孝を盡す
義の成らざる未熟を以て。骨肉にあらざる主君の恩義に感じて。
忠節を盡す事の。罷成べき道理とては。更々無之候。家に在て親
へ不孝の子は。外へ出て主君を取り。奉公致すとても。主君の襟も
とに目をつけ。少しにても左前に成り給ふと見ては。頓て志を變じ
鐔際になめては矢狹間をくゞり。或は敵へ内通降参の不義を仕る
は。古今間ある事にて。恥愼しむべき所に候。初心の武士心得の
ため仍如件。

Even such a cantankerous parent must be reverenced as a parent and his bad temper be appeased and his aged infirmities be sympathized with and regretted, all without showing any signs of annoyance. For exerting oneself to the utmost for such a parent is true filial piety. And a samurai who possesses this spirit when he enters the service of a lord will thoroughly understand the Way of Loyalty and will show it, not only when his master is prosperous but also if he meets adversity. He will not leave his master's side when his hundred horsemen are reduced to ten and this ten to one, but will defend him to the end, regarding his own life as nothing in carrying out a warrior's sworn fealty to his lord.

And so though the terms "parent" and "lord," "filial conduct" and "loyalty," are distinct, in no way do they differ in meaning. The ancients have a saying, "Look for a loyal retainer among the filial"; and it is unreasonable to think that if a man is unfilial to his parents he can at the same time be loyal to his master. For if someone is incapable of carrying out his filial duties to his parents, from whom he sprang, it is most unlikely that he will give loyal service to a lord who is no relation, out of pure gratitude. When he enters a lord's service, an unfilial son of this kind will be critical of any shortcoming of his master. When he does not approve of something, he will throw off his allegiance and slip away at a critical moment or betray his lord by giving himself up to the enemy. Examples can be seen of such disgraceful conduct in all periods, and it is to be shunned with the greatest loathing.

士法

武士道に。二法四段の子細有之候。二法とは常法變法に候。常法の内に士法兵法あり。變法の内に軍法戰法有て。都合四段に候。

先づ士法と申は。朝夕手足を洗ひ。湯風呂にも入て。身を潔く持なし。毎朝髪を結ひ。節々月額をも剃り。時節に應じたる禮服を着し。刀脇差の義は申に及ばず。腰に扇子を離さず。客對のときは。尊卑に隨て相當の禮義を盡し。無益の言語を愼しみ。たとひ一椀の飯を食し。一服の茶を啜るに付ても。其さま拙なからざる樣にと。油斷なく是をたしなみ。其身奉公人ならば。非番休息の透々には只居を致さず。書を讀字を書き。武家の古實古法を心にかけ。行住坐臥の行義作法。流石武士と見ゆる樣に。身を持なす義に候。

Samurai Ordinances

In Bushido there are two ordinances and four sections. The two ordinances are the ordinary and the extraordinary. The former is divided into two sections about the officials and about the soldiers, while the latter is similarly divided into those of army affairs and of battle affairs.

As to the section about the samurai officials, they should wash their hands and feet night and morning, take a hot bath, and in that way keep themselves clean. A samurai must do his hair every morning and keep the hair properly shaved from his forehead. Then he must always wear the ceremonial dress proper to the occasion and, of course, wear his two swords as well as carry a fan in his sash. When he receives a guest he must treat him with the etiquette due to his rank and must refrain from idle talk. Even in taking a bowl of rice or a cup of tea it must be done correctly without sloppiness and with no lack of vigilance. If he is serving in some capacity when he is off duty he must not lounge about doing nothing but should read and practice writing, storing his mind with the ancient history and precepts of the warrior houses. In short, he should conduct himself at all times so that his manners are those proper to a samurai.

次に兵法と申は。腰刀の勝負を最初と致し。鑓をつかひ馬に乘。弓を射鐵砲を發し。其外何によらず武藝とさへあれば。數寄好みて稽古仕り。修練を極めて。其身の覺悟と致す義に候。右士法兵法の二段の修行さへ相調候へば。常法に於ては何の不足も無之候に付。大抵の人の眼には。拔も好武士かな。よき使ひ料かなと見え申ものに候。然りといへども。武士はもと變の役人に候。世の騒動の砌は。日比の士法をばしばらく取置。常には御主君殿樣と申御方を。御大將と申し。家中大小の士の義は。軍兵士卒と呼び。上も下も禮服を脱ぎ捨て。身には甲冑を着。手に兵仗を提げて。敵地へ進み向ふ樣體をさして軍陣と申候。

是に付て種々の仕樣仕形の習ひ事あるを。名付て軍法と申候。是を知らずしては叶ふべからず候。次に戰法と申は。敵味方出會て。既に一戰に及ぶ刻。味方備の立配り。人數の扱ひ。圖に當る時は勝利をえ。圖に當らざる時は勝利を失ひ。敗北に及び候。其仕樣仕形に習ひ口訣あるを。名付て戰法と申候。是亦知らずしては叶ふべからず候。變法に二段ありと申すは此事に候。

Next comes the section on soldiers. This concerns the exercise of fencing, spear practice, horsemanship, and shooting with bow and matchlock-musket, together with everything else that pertains to the military art that must be enthusiastically studied and practiced so that all will be disciplined and resolute. And if these two codes of the samurai official and the soldier are well understood, the ordinary ordinance may be considered complete, and this would appear to most people to be sufficient for the good warrior or official. Yet a samurai is an official for extraordinary conditions, and when the country is in a state of disorder he must lay aside the ordinary rule for samurai life and serve under his lord as commander, the greater and lesser retainers becoming officers and soldiers. Then all put away their ceremonial attire and don their armor and take arms in hand to advance into the enemy territory.

It is the various methods of arranging matters on such a campaign that are known as the rule of army affairs, and this is a thing that must be known. Then comes the rule of battle affairs, which is the method of handling the army when it comes into contact with the enemy to give battle. If things go according to plan there is victory; and if not, there is defeat. This, too, is a thing whose secrets must be understood.

右常法變法四段の修行成就の武士をさして。上品の士とは申にて
候。常法の二段相調ひ候得ば。一騎前の勤めに於ては事濟候得
共。變法の二段に未熟にては。士大將者頭物奉行等は勤り不申
候。依て爰を分別致し。とても武士を立罷在に付ては。士法兵法
の義は申に及ばず。軍法戰法の奥秘まで修行致し。一度上品の士
と不罷成しては。指置まじきものをと心懸。肝要の所に候。初心の
武士心えの爲仍如件。

不忘勝負

武士たらむものは。行住座臥二六時中。勝負の氣を忘れず。心に
置を以て。肝要と仕り候。本朝の義は異國にかはり。いか程輕き百
姓町人職人體の者たりとも。似合相應に錆脇指の一腰づゝは相た
しなみ罷在候。是日本武國の風俗に候。然りといへども。三民の輩
は。武を家業とは不仕候。武門に於ては。末々の小者中間の類に
至るまでも。常に脇指を放してはならぬ作法に候。況や士分上の輩
としては。片時が間も腰に刃物を離しては不罷成事に候。去に依
て心懸深き武士は。常に湯あび申所まで。刃びき刀。或は木刀など
を指置候。

And what is called a first-class samurai is one who is skilled in all four sections of these two ordinances. To be experienced only in the two sections of the ordinary one may be sufficient for the duties of the average cavalier, or mounted horseman, but no one who is ignorant of the extraordinary sections can become a commander or high officer, such as *monogashira* or *bugyo*. It is therefore most important that all samurai should realize that they cannot rise to the highest positions without profound study of the extraordinary ordinance.

Never Neglect the Offensive Spirit

It is most important that a samurai should always be alert to going on the offensive at any time and in all matters. For our country is different from other lands, in that even the least of the people—that is, the farmers, merchants, and artisans—should all hold close some rusty blade, wherein is revealed the warrior spirit of this Empire of Nippon. These three classes are not soldiers by profession, though. Still, it is the custom in military families for even the lowliest servants of the samurai never to be without a short sword, even for a moment. The higher samurai must always wear their sash. And some very meticulous ones wear a blunt sword or a wooden one even when they go to the bath.

我家内にてさへ其心懸有之上は。ましてや私宅を離れて他所へ罷越には。往還の道すがらより。其行たる向に於ても酒狂人。又はいか様の馬鹿者に出逢て。不慮の仕合に及ぶ義も有まじきに非ず候。古人の詞にも。門を出れば敵を見るがごとくなど有之候。其身武士として。腰に刀劍を帶るからは。片時が間も勝負の氣を忘るべき様は是なく候。勝負の氣を忘れざる時は。おのづから死を心にあつるの實にも相叶ひ候。腰に刀劍をさしはさむといへども。勝負の氣を心に置ざる士は。取りも直さず武士の皮をかぶりたる百姓町人にて候。初心の武士心得のため仍如件。

出家士

昔より出家士と申ならはし候が。實も相似寄たる様子も有之候。たとへば禪家に於て。何藏主何首座など名付たるは。是皆平僧にて。武家にとりては。外様奉公を仕る。組付の平士と同格に候。次に一段級を踰え。單寮西堂など申候は。武家に於て目付役。番士の組頭。或は徒士頭等の諸役者にひとしきものに候。扨亦同じ出家ながらも。色衣の法服を身にまとひ。手に拂子執柄を持て。大勢の大衆を攝得致し候を。長老和尚と申候は。武家に於ては自分指物をさし。或は羽織采拜を許されて。士卒を引廻し。軍の下知をなす。士大將足輕大將。扨は弓矢の六奉行など申す武士に同じき様子に候。

And if this is their way in the house, it is even more necessary when one leaves it to go somewhere else, because on the road you may meet some drunkard or other fool who might suddenly start a quarrel. There is an old saying, "When you leave your gate, act as though an enemy was in sight." So when one is a samurai and wears a sword in his sash he must never forget this spirit of the offensive. And, when this is so, his mind is firmly fixed on death. But the samurai who does not maintain this aggressive spirit, even though he wears a sword at his side, is nothing but a farmer or a shopkeeper in a warrior's skin.

Recluse Samurai

From ancient times it has been customary for samurai to become hermits, and indeed there is much resemblance between the two. For instance, among the Zen monks there are those called *zosu* and *shuza*, who are ordinary young shave-headed monks with the same standing as the outside retainers among the military class who are merely foot soldiers of the companies. Then come the *tanryo* and *seido,* a rank higher, who are more or less the equivalent of the *metsuke* (Censor) or Captains of the Guards or Captains of Infantry among the samurai. Among these same recluses are some called *choro* or *osho*, who wear colored robes and carry a fly-whisk staff in their hand and lord it over the common folk just like the Commander of the Samurai or Commander of the Infantry. And also there are the Six *Bugyo* of the Archers, who are privileged to have their own flag and great-coat and baton, and who issue orders to the army and take command when in the field.

但學問の務め方に於ては。釋門の同宿共の務め方に合せては。武家の同宿は遙かに劣りて覺え候。子細を申すに。釋門の作法は。平僧にて罷在候内に。師匠の手前を離れ。諸寺諸山を遍歴仕り。餘多の學匠明師にも出會。參禪參得の功を積み。たとひ單寮西堂。又は長老和尚に經上り。本寺本山の住職を勤むる身と罷成候ても。少しも恥かしからぬ様に。學問を致し究めて。出世の時の至るを相待罷在候。

武家に於ても。左様にこそ有り度事に候所。無役の平士にて。外様奉公仕り。隙にて罷在候者も。似合相當の祿有之。衣食住の三つに於て。何の不足も無之故。いまだ年若き者も妻子を持ち。朝寝書寝を業と致し。士の常法たる。兵法をさへ學び務めず候からは。ましてや手遠なる。軍法戦法の事は。思ひがけもなくて。

一日ぬらりに年月を送る内に。そろそろ髭白毛も生ひ出。額口も禿上りて。何様尤らしき年齢に見ゆるを以て。役ぬけの撰擧に預り。譬へば使番などになり候ても。早當座から行あたり。同役仲間の介抱を以て。何とか相勤め罷在内に。常に無之遠國使など有之時は。俄に胸をつき。族行の支度にとりまぜて。先輩の口傳を受。古來の控覺書など借用して。漸々と其場を勤め候は。幸にして免れたると申すものにて。本道の事とは申されず候。

Only in learning do these communities of recluses seem to me to be far superior to those of the samurai. The reason is that it is the way of ordinary monks to leave their teachers and travel around the country from one monastery to another for study. In so doing they meet many distinguished scholars and accumulate merits in the practice of meditation and virtue. And when they rise to be *tanryo* and *seido,* and even *choro* and *osho,* and become the abbots of great temples and monasteries, they are still not in ashamed in the slightest to continue their study and research in order that they may be worthy of promotion.

So, also, should I like to see it among the samurai. But even ordinary samurai without office who do outside service and have a good deal of free time have actually a relatively high income and are well provided with the necessities of life. Some who are still young even have wives and children, and their only occupation seems to be taking morning and afternoon naps. They have not even studied the two sections of the ordinary ordinance for samurai, much less have they acquired any knowledge of the more obscure extraordinary ordinance.

And in this way do they pass the months and years in idleness until their beards grow white and their heads bald. Then, when they seem to be about the age for it, they are assigned to the status of those who are relieved of office, and if for instance they should act as *tsukai-ban,* or envoy, they go off at once and get the assistance of some colleague and so carry out their affairs. But if they are sent to some distant province, then they feel flustered and distracted by the preparations for the journey. When they do take up their duties they are barely able to carry them out by relying on instructions from seniors and borrowing books of reference, a state of things that cannot be considered the proper way.

子細を申に。武家の諸役儀大形定り有ものなれば。其身無役の
内。連々心にかけ。役義馴たる功者に参會の序毎には。無益の雑
談を相止め。向後の心付にも可罷成と。思ひ寄たる事共をば。幾
度も問尋ねて。委細に聞覺え。或は古き控覺書。繪圖等までも借り
あつめて寫し置。勤方の大筋を呑込候得ば。何時何役に成り候て
も。務り易き道理に候。

其上先輩同役に便りて事を習ひ。介抱に預りて事を濟すも。常式
の時の儀に候。萬一世の變に至り候ては。人の介抱引廻しに預る
事はならざる事に候間。善くも惡くも我獨分別にて。埒を明るより
外は無之候。就中軍中の使役と申すは。敵の人數の多少。陣取備
立の善惡。城の堅固不堅固。或は地形の利不利。合戰勝負の見切
までをも。相心得ずしては不叶候。去るに依て。軍使役の儀は。古
來よりむつかしきものに申し習はし候。然れども使役の儀は。たと
ひ我が物見に相違の儀有之候ても。多分は其身壹人の不覺越度
にて事濟申候。足輕大將より上の役儀に備り。采拜を取て人數を
引廻し候に至ては。味方諸勢の死生に懸り申候。然るに其勘辨な
く。なまじひに采拜免許の役儀に高ぶり。諸士の座上を潰し候は。
沙汰の限り不屆の仕合に候。

For as the duties of samurai are practically all fixed, they should consider those duties when they have nothing to do. When they meet officers of ability and experience, they should cease idle talk and make a point of inquiring from them about matters on which they anticipate they will need advice. They must acquaint themselves with all the facts and must collect and copy old books and plans so that they are well informed about every aspect of their duty. Then, whatever they are ordered to do at any time, they will find it easy to undertake.

And if they depend on their seniors and colleagues for information and perform duties with their help, this may do for ordinary ones. But in the rare case when something unusual happens, they may not be able to get any assistance, and then, for good or evil, must depend on their own ability to solve the problem. And an Inspector of the Forces must know all about such things as the numbers of an enemy, the best place to make camp and arrange the troops, the strength of castles, the advantages or disadvantages of geographical position, and the probability of victory. So it is that from ancient times this office has been regarded as a difficult one. However, if an Inspector makes a miscalculation in his views, the matter will most likely end only in blame for him, whereas those above the rank of Infantry Commander (*ashigaru taisho*), who wield the marshal's baton and have actual control over the troops, are responsible for the lives of all the men in their army. Therefore it is a most reprehensible thing that men should disgrace such a high command by swaggering about without any proper knowledge or mental ability.

禪僧のうへにては。平僧の時宗旨の學問に怠り。出世の年臘に至り。頭の禿たる廉を以て。長老和尚に經上り。身に色衣を纏ひ。手に拂子を握り。餘多の大衆を攝得いたすに均しき樣子に候。但右の賣僧和尚。晴なる法席に臨みて何ぞ不埒有之候得ば。大衆一統の物笑ひとなり。其身一人赤恥をかきて。引込申ばかりの儀にて。大衆へ懸る難儀とては少しも無之候。それとは違ひ。武家に於て和尚役を務る武士。采拝を振損じ候時は。味方士卒の身命に懸り。害を爲す事大に候。爰を能々分別仕り。無役にて身の暇有之砌。軍法戰法の修行を極め。采拝所持の職たり共務り兼る儀無之樣。學問修行尤に候。初心の武士心得のため仍如件。

It is as though among the Zen monks one who neglected his studies when he was a junior should, merely by virtue of a bald head and old age, be advanced to the rank of *choro* or *osho,* wear gorgeous robes and carry the fly-whisk, and flaunt authority over multitudes of his brethren. If an unworthy monk of this type were to be wrongly exalted to such high position, he would find himself the laughingstock of the whole community, and be publicly shamed and have to resign, so that he would do no real harm to the order. But it is different with samurai who are promoted to similar high office and are incompetent to command, for they jeopardize the lives of all under them, and the loss they can cause is very great. Therefore, they must be extremely diligent to study, whenever they have any spare time, so they can gain a thorough knowledge of the ordinances of the army and of battle. For both study and practice are most necessary to one who holds a high command.

義不義

武士たらむものは。義不義の二つをとくと心に會得仕り。專ら義を
務めて。不義を戒しむべきとさへ覺悟仕り候へば。武士道は相立
申候。義不義と申は善惡の二つにして。義は即善。不義は即惡に
候。凡人として善惡不義の辨への無と申事は無之候得共。義を行
ひ善に勸む事は。窮屈にして太儀に思はれ。不義を行ひ惡を為す
事は。面白く心安きを以て。ひたすら不義惡事の方へのみ流れて。
義を行ひ善に勸む事は。いやに罷威事に候。其身一向のうつけも
のにて。善惡義不義の差別無之は論に及ばず候。既に不義惡事
と了簡をば仕りながら。義理を違へて不義を行ひ候は。武士の意
地に非ず。近頃未練の至りに候。其本は物に堪忍情の薄きがゆゑ
とも可申候。堪忍情の薄きと申せば。聞よき樣に候得共。其根元を
尋候へば。臆病よりおこる事に候。去るに依て。武士は常に不義を
愼しみ。義に從ふを以て肝要とは申にて候。

拠義を行ふに付て。三段の樣子有之候。譬ば我近付の者と同道し
て。他所へ行事あるに。其つれの者百兩の金子を所持致し。是を
懷中いたしありくも苦勞に候間。後刻罷歸候まで。爰許に預け置度
と申候に付。其金子を預り。人の不知樣に納め置て。其者とつれ
立參りたる向に於て。件の連の者大食傷。又は卒中風などの急病
を煩ひ出し。即時に相果候義有之時は。右金子を預けたるも預り
たるも。外に知りたる者とては壹人も無之候。然るに拠も笑止なる
仕合かなと。痛ましく思ふ心より外には毛頭も邪念なく。右預り置
たる金子の義を。其ものゝ親類へ申理り。早速返し遣はすは是眞
によく義を行ふ人と可申候。

Right and Wrong

He who is a warrior should possess a thorough understanding of right and wrong. If he knows how to do the one and avoid the other, then he will have attained to Bushido. Right and wrong are nothing but good and evil. Though I would not deny that there is a slight difference between the terms, to act rightly and do good is difficult and is regarded as boring, whereas to act wrongly and do evil is easy and amusing. Naturally, therefore, most incline to the wrong or evil and tend to dislike the right and good. But to be thus unstable and make no distinction between right and wrong is contrary to reason. Anyone who understands this distinction and yet does what is wrong is no proper samurai, but is a raw and untaught person. And the cause of it is poor self-control. Though this may not sound so bad, if we look into its origin we find it arises from cowardice. That is why I maintain that it is essential for a samurai to refrain from wrong and cling fast to what is right.

Now in the matter of doing right, there are three degrees. Say that a man's neighbor who is going on a journey has a hundred *ryo* of gold that, to avoid the trouble of carrying it with him, he deposits with this man until he comes back, and he does so without telling anyone about it. Then on the journey this neighbor is suddenly taken ill from overeating, or a stroke, or something of the sort, and dies of it, so that there is nobody at all who knows anything about the money. But say that the other man, purely out of sympathy and compassion and nothing else, and without a single evil thought, immediately informs the relatives and returns all the money to them. This is truly a man who does what is right.

次は右の金主と申は。大抵の知人までにて。左のみ入魂と申にも
無之。預りたり金子の義は。外に知りたる者なければ。何方より問
尋ねのあるべき事にも非ず。折しも我が手前も不如意なれば。幸
の義なり。是は沙汰なしに致し置ても苦しかるまじきかと。邪念の
さし出候を。扨もむさき意地出たる物かなと。我と我心を恥しめ。
急度分別を致しかへ。件の金子を返すは。是を心に恥て義を行ふ
人と可申候。

又其次は。右の金子預り置候を。妻子召使のものの中に於て。壹
人にても存じたるもの有之に付。其者のおもわくを恥。後日の沙汰
を憚りて。其金を返すは。是人に恥て義を行ふ人と可申候。但し如
此なるは。一向に知りたる人さへ無くば如何あるべきや。去りなが
ら。是も亦義を知て行ふ人に非ずとは申がたく候。

In the second case, suppose that the neighbor who owned the money had only a few acquaintances and was not a close friend to anybody, so that no one would know about the money he had left with the other man and therefore no one would be likely to inquire about it. If the other man was not very well off, he might rightly regard it as a lucky windfall and think it would hurt no one to be silent about it and so keep it for himself. But then a sudden shame would come over him for having even dreamed of such a wicked idea, and he would dismiss the thought at once and return the money. This is doing right on account of shame that proceeds from one's mind.

Then there is the third case where somebody in his house—either one of his family or of his servants—knows about this money, and he is ashamed of what that person may think or what may be said of him in the future and so returns it to the rightful owner. This is one who does right from shame connected with other people. But here we may wonder what he would do if nobody knew anything about it. Still, we can hardly pronounce him a person who, though he does not know what is right, does it anyway.

總じて義を行ふ修行の心得と申は。我が妻子召使を初め。身に親しき輩の下墨を第一に恥慎しみ。それより廣く他人の誹り嘲りを。恥入て不義をなさず。義を行ひつけ候得ば。自然とそれが習と成て。後々は義に從ふことを好み。不義を行ふ事をいやに存ずる意地合に罷成候物に候。

抑又武勇の道に於ても。生得の勇者と申すは。戰場に臨み。いか程矢鐵炮の劇しき場所をも何とも思はず。忠と義との二つにはまる。其身を的になして進み行心の勇氣は。形にも顯はるゝ故。其ふり合の美事さ。兎角申されざる物に候。或は偖も危なき事かな。これはいかゞ致して善からむと。胸も轟き。膝節も顫ふといへども。人も行るればこそ行中に。我獨行ずしては。味方の諸人の見る目もあれば。後日に至りて口のきかれぬ所なりと。是非なく思ひ切。勇者と相ならびて進み行ものも有之。右に申す生得の勇者と並べては。遙に劣り候得共。幾度も左樣の首尾に出合て。場を踏み重ね物馴候へば。後々は心も定まり。生得の勇者にもさして劣る事なき。譽れの剛の武士とも罷成候。

然れば義を行ひ勇を勵むに付ても。兎角恥を知ると申より外に。心得とては無之候。よし人は不義ともいへ。大事なしと云て不義を行ひ。抑も腰ぬけかなと申て笑はゞ笑へ。大事なしと云て臆病をはたらく者には。何を申教ゆべき樣も無之候。初心の武士心得のため仍如件。

Generally speaking, though, the rule for the practice of right conduct is that we would first feel shame if we earned the contempt of our family and servants and friends, and then feel the scorn of the wider circle of our acquaintances and of outsiders, and thus we will shun the wrong and do right. This will then, naturally, become a habit and in time we will acquire the disposition to prefer the right and dislike the wrong.

When it comes to courage in battle, he who is born brave will think nothing of going into battle where he might come under a hot fire of arrows and bullets. Devoted to loyalty and duty, he will make his body a target and press on, presenting by his splendid valor an indescribably fine example to all who see him. But by contrast, there may be one whose knees tremble and whose heart quakes as he wonders how he can possibly acquit himself honorably in all this danger. He goes on anyway, because he is ashamed to be the only one to falter under the eyes of his comrades as they advance, and because he fears loss of reputation in the future. So he hardens his resolve and forges on, right behind the naturally valiant one. Thus, though he may be vastly inferior to the born brave, after several of these experiences he becomes used to it and gains his footing. Eventually his courage is confirmed, and he grows into a warrior who is by no means inferior to the born fearless.

So both in doing right and in producing valor there is no other way but a sense of shame. For if people say of wrong that it does not matter and then do it, and just laugh if they see a coward and say that it does not matter either, how can this kind of person possibly be disciplined?

勇者

武士道において肝要と仕り候は。忠義勇の三つに止り申候。忠勤の武士。節義の武士。勇剛の武士を申候。此忠義勇の三徳を。一人に兼備へたる武士をさして。上品の士と申候。去れば百千の武士の中において。上品の士と申は稀なるものに候。扨忠勤の武士と。節義の武士との見分けは。常々の行跡にも顕はれ。知れ易き道理に候。勇者の義は。治世の今。無事の時代には。知れ兼可申やとの不審も有之候得共。左様には無之候。子細を申に。凡勇氣と申すものは。身に甲冑をよそひ。手に鎗薙刀を持て。戦場に臨み。勝負を争ふ時節に至り。初て顕はるゝにては更々無之候。平生畳の上において。是は勇者。是は不勇者と申す見分けは。成程相知れ申ものにて候。

生得の勇者と申すものは。主親へ忠孝を勵み。少しにても身の暇あれば。學文に心を寄せ。武藝の稽古も怠る事なく。身の奢りを愼み。一錢の費をも厭ふ。扨は吝くきたなき心かと見れば左はなく。致さで叶はぬ事には。金銀を惜氣なく出し。或は主君の御法度。或は親々の嫌ふ事とさへあれば。何程我が行度と思ふ所へも行ず。止にくき事をも止めて。兎にも角にも主親の心に背かず。身命を全く保ちて。是非一度は大功を立んと思ふを以て。常々の養生深く。喰度物をもひかへ。飲たき物をも飲まず。人間第一の惑なる。色情をも愼しみ遠ざけ。其外萬事の上に付て。物によく堪へ忍ぶ意地のあるは。是皆勇者のきつかけに候。

Bravery

The three qualities of Loyalty, Right Conduct, and Bravery are essential for Bushido. We speak of the loyal warrior, the righteous warrior, and the brave warrior. He who is endowed with all three of these virtues is considered a warrior of the highest class. But among the myriads of samurai it is rare to find one of this kind. Now it may not be hard to distinguish the loyal warrior from a righteous one by observing their ordinary, everyday conduct. But it may be doubted whether, in times of peace and quiet like the present, it will be so easy to single out the valiant one. This, however, is not so, for bravery does not show itself first when a man puts on armor and takes spear and halberd in hand and goes out to battle. You can see whether he is brave when he is sitting on the mats leading his ordinary life.

For he who is born brave will be loyal and filial to his lord and his parents, and whenever he has any leisure he will use it for study. Neither will he neglect to practice the military arts. He will be strictly on his guard against habitual laziness and will be very careful how he spends every penny. If you think this shows detestable stinginess you will be mistaken, since he spends freely when necessary. He does nothing that is contrary to the ordinances of his lord or that is disliked by his parents, however much he may wish to. And so, being ever obedient to his lord and his parents, he preserves his life in the hope of someday doing a deed of outstanding merit, moderating his appetite for eating and drinking and avoiding overindulgence in sex, which is the greatest delusion of mankind, all so that he may preserve his body in health and strength. For in these, as in all other things, it is firm self-control that is the beginning of valor.

抑又不勇者と申は主君をも親をも。上べばかり敬ふふりを致し。信實に大切と存ずる意地は無之。主君の法度。親々のいやがる事といふ愼みもなく。行まじき所へも狼狽ありき。仕るまじき事も仕り。萬に氣隨を先だて。朝寢晝寢を好みて。學文をば大きに嫌ひ。

武藝を務るとても。何一色取しめて稽古致す事もなく。所作も叶はぬ藝白慢の利口だてばかり申し。役にも立ぬ阿房狂ひ。又は榮耀喰ひなどにはいか程も物を入れ。知行の物成切符をも。跡先の考へなしに遣ひ散し。致さで叶はぬ事には至て嗇く。親の讓りに受たる古具足毛切れ仕り。塗の剥候を。修復致すべき心掛さへ無之仕合なれば。ましてや外の武具馬具の不足を改めて。新たに支度するなどは思ひも寄ず。

But he who is not brave will appear to be only superficially loyal and filial to his lord and parents and will have no sincere intention of remaining so. Indifferent to his lord's rules and his parents' dislikes, he is given to unchaste strolling where he should not go, doing what he ought not do, and in everything putting his own wishes first. He loves to sleep both in the morning and in the afternoon, and he especially dislikes having to study.

As for the military arts, he knows all about them but hates to practice them, instead merely boasting about his skill at what he cannot do and feeling full of enthusiasm about some useless undertaking. He spends any amount of money on sumptuous feasting, and frivols away his allowance and mortgages his salary with no foresight at all. But where he should spend he is stingy and will not even bother to repair the chipped lacquer and broken cords of the worn-out armor he inherits from his father. Much less will he buy any new suits or any horse saddles or equipment to make up for losses.

其身病者にては。主君へ奉公も叶はず。親々の氣遣ひ苦勞になる
といふ勘辨もなく。大食大酒の上色情に耽り。我と我が壽命に鑵
子を懸る如くなるは。是皆物に堪忍ぶことの成り兼る。柔弱未練の
心より起る義なれば。是を不勇者。臆病武士のきつかけと目利し
て。大方外れは無之候。爰を以て勇者も不勇者も。疊の上に於て。
成程相知れ候とは申にて候。初心の武士心得のため仍如件。

禮敬

忠孝の二つの道は。武士の身の上に限りたる義にては無之。農工
商とてもかはる義は無之候。然りといへども。三民のうへには。譬
へば人の子人の下人たる者が。主親と同座を致すに。膝を組。ぬ
き入手を致し。物を云ふにも手をつくこともなく。下に坐して居る主
親へ。立ながら物を申し。其外萬事に付。無禮不作法多けれども。
それには搆ひなく。唯主親を大切に思ふ志の誠をさへ盡し候得
ば。事濟申候は。是三民の輩の忠孝に候。

武士道に於ては。たとひいか程心に忠孝を守り候ても。其形にお
いて。主を敬ひ親を尊ぶの禮儀なくては。道に叶ひたるとは申され
ず候。但主君の御事は申すに及ばす。親々へ對し候ても。目の前に
於ての慮外緩怠は。武士を立る程のものは。可仕樣無之候。主親
の目通りを離れ。陰うしろに於ても。聊疎略を致す事なく。陰日向
なきを以て。武士の忠孝とは申にて候。

His health is too poor for him to serve his lord properly, and he does not even think about the trouble and anxiety this causes his parents. He eats and drinks too much and is excessive in sexual matters. This using up and filing away of his physical powers and longevity is due to nothing but a weak and unschooled mind incapable of self-control. We would not be far wrong in diagnosing this as the source of cowardice in a samurai. In this way can the valiant samurai be distinguished from the cowardly one, even while sitting on the mats at home.

Respect

The two Ways of Loyalty and Filial Duty are not limited to the samurai. They are equally obligatory for the farmer, artisan, and merchant classes. But among these classes, for example, a child or servant while sitting with his parent or master may have his legs crossed or his arms akimbo, or he may speak to them standing while they are sitting, or may do various other disrespectful and impolite things and it does not matter. If he is genuinely sincere in his filial feelings and truly cherishes his master or parent, that is all that is expected in the case of these three classes.

But in Bushido, however loyal and filial a man may be in his heart, if he lacks the correct etiquette and manners by which respect is shown to lord or parent, he cannot be regarded as living in conformity with it. Any negligence of this kind, whether it be toward his lord or toward his parents, is no conduct for anyone who thinks of himself as a samurai. And even when out of their sight and in private, a warrior must never become lax and be either black or white in his loyalty and filial duty.

何れの所に寝臥を仕り候共。主君の御座の方へは。かりにも我足をさし向けず。卷藁を立弓を射るにも。御座の方へは矢落をなさず。鎗長刀を懸置にも。切先をさし向けず。其外主君の御噂に懸りたる義を耳に聞か。又は我が口より詞に出す時は。寝ころび居ても起上り。平座に居ても居直る類をこそ。武士道と申べけれ。

然るを主君の御座の方と存じながらも。臑をさし向け。臥て居ながら主君の御噂を申出。或は親の自筆の手紙を得ても。戴きて見る心付もなく。大膝を組て居ながらも。臥りながらも。披見を遂げ。側らへ投ほふり。或は引裂て煙管行灯の掃除を致す類ひ。皆後闇き所存に候。左様なる心立の者は。他所他門の者に出會ては主人の家の宜しからざる義を。かぞへあげて演説仕り。或は一向の他人にても。我に念比らしく言てくれる者さへあれば是を悦び。親兄弟の悪しき噂をも。包まず泄さず語り出て。嘲り誹謗仕るものに候。去るに依て。いつぞの程には。主親の罰を蒙り。何ぞ大なる禍に出會。武士の冥理に盡たる死を致すか。たとひ生ても。生甲斐なき風情となり果るか。如何様すなほにて生涯を送る義は。決して無之道理に候。

Wherever he may be lying down or sleeping, his feet must never for an instant be pointing in the direction of his lord's presence. If he sets up a straw bale for archery practice anywhere, the arrows must never fall toward the place where his lord is. Similarly, when he puts down his spear or halberd their points must never be in that direction. And if he hears any talk about his lord, or if anything about him escapes his own lips, if he is lying down he must spring up, and if he is resting at ease he must sit up straight. For that is the Way of the Samurai.

Other things that show a samurai's stupid lack of consideration are pointing the elbow toward where he knows the lord is, talking about him while sprawling on the mats, and throwing aside or tearing up a letter by his parents or using part of it to clean a pipe or night-light. People of such mentality are likely, when they meet outsiders, to speak ill of their lord's affairs. And if anyone, even a complete outsider, comes and talks slyly to them, they will be quite pleased and will not hesitate to pour out a lot of scandal about their parents or elder brothers and speak ill of them and talk abusively about them. Surely they will meet with punishment from their lord, or with some other misfortune at one time or other, and their end will not be one befitting a warrior. But even if they live to an old age, it will be a worthless existence, certainly not a normal one of peace and prosperity.

昔し慶長の頃福島左衛門大夫政則の足輕大將。可兒才藏と申武
勇の士有之。藝州廣嶋の城内。黒金門を預り。一日一夜詰切の番
所を勤るに。其身極老なれば。休息のため寝ころび居たる所へ。政
則の側に召使ひ玉ふ小坊主。鷹の鶉を持參致し。是は殿様の御拳
の鳥にて候間。被遣候との御意の旨申述る。才藏是を承り。其まゝ
起上り傍に脱置たる袴を着し。本丸の方へ向ひて是を戴き。御禮
の義は。只今罷上りて可申上なり。

扨おのれめ。如何に倅なればとて。大なる空氣奴かな。殿の御意な
らば。先づ殿の御意あるぞと申聞。身共が其用意したる上にて達
すべきを。左はなくして。身共に寝ながら殿の御意をよくも聞せた
り。おのれ倅にてなくば仕形もあれ共。小僧の義なれば免すぞと申
て。大きに叱りければ。小僧肝を潰し。急ぎ立歸りて。兒姓共の中
にて右の次第を語るを。政則聞玉ひ件の小僧を呼出し尋られけれ
ば。才藏が申分殘らず申すに付。それはおのれが不調法なれば。
才藏が腹立尤なり。藝備兩國の士共を。殘らず才藏が心の如く致
して欲しきものかな。それにては何事も成るにと。政則被申ける由
に候。初心の武士心得のため仍如件。

In days gone by, in the Keicho era, there lived a valiant warrior named Kani Saizo, a Commander of Infantry under Fukushima Saemon-taiyu Masanori, who kept watch both day and night by the iron gate of the castle of Hiroshima in Aki. Because Saizo was an old man, he would drop off to sleep at times during his duty, and on one of these occasions a page of Masanori's came to him and brought a young hawk with a message that it was a present from his master. Saizo at once sprang up, put on the *hakama* that he had taken off and laid aside, turned toward Hommaru Palace, and received the hawk, saying that he would immediately call there to return thanks.

Then he went on, "As for you, if you were my son I would call you an idiot, for if you bring a message from our lord you should say so right away, so that I could be prepared for it, and not give it to me without any warning when I am having a nap like this. It is a good thing you are not my son. Since you are only a page, I suppose you know no better, so I will excuse you." The boy hurried away, shaken by this scolding, and told his youthful comrades all about it, so that after a while it came to the ears of Masanori himself. He then called the page and questioned him about it, and when he confirmed the story his master said, "Saizo was right in being angry at such disrespect. I wish that all the samurai of Aki and Bizen had his spirit, for then there would be nothing they could not do."

馬術

昔の武士の義は。弓馬と申候て。大身小身共に弓を射馬に乗を以て。武藝の最上と仕りたる由に候。近代の武士の義は。太刀鎗扱は馬術を。肝要と心懸て稽古仕り候。其外弓鐵炮居合和術など申す。萬つの武藝共に。年若き武士は。朝暮の勤と致し。習び學び尤に候。年ふけ候ては。何を習度と存じ候ても。心に任せぬものにて候。

偖小身の武士は。別して馬をよく乗習ひ。たとひ過もの。又は手を嫌ふ馬といふとも。是をあまさず乗こなし申様にあり度事に候。子細を申すに。乗あひよくて馬形も宜敷馬は。世間に稀に候。たとひ有之候ても。大身武士の乗料となるを以て。小身武士の馬屋に繋ぐ事は成兼申候。其身馬術にさへ達し候へば。是はよき馬なれ共。過物とか。又は一癖有て。人の手を嫌ふ類の馬を見立て。馬代下直に買求め。乗料と致す時は。いつとても身上に過たる馬を持て罷在候。總じて馬の毛色毛疵を吟味致すも。大身武士の事にて候。小身の武士は。我が性に合ぬ毛色の馬をも厭はず。毛疵有て。人のいやがる馬をも嫌ふことなく。馬さへよくば。求めて繋ぐ心得尤に候。

Horsemanship

In ancient times, all samurai, both high and low, considered archery and horsemanship to be the first of the military arts. More recently, they prefer to practice with the sword and spear and then to value skill in riding. Moreover, it is highly appropriate that youthful samurai should continue to train daily in shooting with the bow and matchlock-musket, in drawing the sword, and in *jujitsu* besides other martial arts, because when they grow older they will not have the time to practice what they wish.

So I would like to see the young samurai pay particular attention to horsemanship, and especially to get used to riding those horses that have faults and hate to be ridden. Good horses and those easy to ride are comparatively rare, since they are acquired by those of high rank and not likely to be found in the stables of the smaller fry. But if a man is a fine horseman and sees a mount that is quite a good one but has some defect or a bad habit, or that likes to toss its rider, he can acquire it for a reasonable sum. Thus, with his horse allowance, he can be mounted considerably above his station. Points like the color or quality of a horse's coat can only affect those of high rank. The small retainer cannot afford to despise an animal because he does not like its color or because its hair is poor, but if it is a good horse he had better buy it and keep it.

むかし信州村上家に。額岩寺と申て。三百騎計の大將にて。弓矢
功者の武士有之。自分の乘料家中の馬共に。世の人の大に嫌ふ
毛疵といへども。少しも忌ことなく。求め繋ぐ家風に致しなし。家中
の諸士に馬場責をさする事なく。五十騎も百騎も城下の廣野へ罷
出。額岩寺眞先に進で。原中を縱横十文字に馳廻り。馬より落るか
と見れば其まゝ飛乘り。乘るかと思へば則飛下り候義を。自由に致
すを以て。よき乘手と申して譽之候。去るに依て。其時代甲州武田
の家中に於ても。信州額岩寺が如くなる敵へは。大物見必ず遠慮
との取沙汰致し候。是額岩寺身にとりて。大き成譽に候。

Long ago, in the province of Shinano, there lived a certain Kakuganji of the Murakami house who was captain of a band of three hundred horsemen, good archers all. He made it a family custom to select his horses only from those that others rejected for some defect in their appearance. He did not bother his men with practice on the racecourse but took them out by fifty or a hundred into the rough ground around the castle town where there was plenty of space. He put himself at the head of his men and galloped them around in all directions, up and down and cross-country. Some of them even liked to partially dismount and strike the ground with their feet while their horses were going hard, then jump back up into the saddle. They rode so well that they made a great name for themselves. And even Takeda of Kai learned to regard these men of Shinano as foes not to be defied without fear of being punished. This proved to be a great tribute to Kakuganji's training.

凡武士の戦場へ乗る馬は。中の上肝にして。高は壹寸より三寸ま
で。頭持は中頭にて。後脚は中の後脚とこそ申傳へ候。然るに乗替
もたぬ。小身武士の壹疋馬を。上肝にして。大高なるを欲しがり。
頭持はいかほども高きに厭かず。後脚は一間後脚など申て。何程
も廣きを悦び。前を取らせむとては腕の筋をのべ。尾をささせじと
ては尾筋を切り。生れもつかぬ片輪馬となして悦び候は。悉皆武
士道不案内より起る物數寄に候。子細を申に。四足の筋をのべた
る馬は。山坂へ懸り。長途を乗。或は川を渉す時。早く草臥て用に
立ず。尾筋をのべたる馬は。溝堀切などを乗越るに。定りて尻懸は
づれ。後脚の廣過たるは。細道を乗るに宜しからずと申傳へ候。

且又武士の馬數寄にも。善惡の二つ有之候。昔の武士の馬數寄
と申すは。具足を着し。指物をさし。身重く成ての懸引は。馬に非ず
しては不叶候。然れば我が兩足のかはりを勤る馬也。其上事の様
子により。馬も深手を負て。命を落す義も有まじきに非ず。畜生な
がら不便の至りと思ふを以て。常の飼料なではたけにも念を入れ。
心を用ひたる事にて候。今時の馬數寄と申すは。癖馬を下直に買
求めて。其癖を乗直し。或は田舎立の駒を見出して。足をのり付。
望む者を待て。高直段に賣拂ふを以て。本意と仕り候。是は伯樂
中次の意地合なれば。一向馬數寄をせぬには劣りに候。初心の武
士心得のため仍如件。

Now, a warrior needs for battle a horse about one to three inches above medium height, with a fair-sized head and hindquarters according to tradition. But for a small retainer who has no spare mount it is better that his one horse should be decidedly tall. He should not mind its head being high, and he should rejoice at the width of its hind end, the kind that is called a six-foot rump. But to like such unnatural and deforming tricks as stretching the leg sinews to give a longer stride, or cutting those of the tail to prevent its being raised, is to show a craving for eccentricity that is entirely inconsistent with Bushido. A horse whose leg sinews are unnaturally stretched will tire quickly and is useless for a long journey uphill or for crossing rivers. And one with its tail sinews cut is apt to slip his harness when jumping over a ditch or canal. But a too broad rump is said not to be good for navigating a narrow path.

There are two ways for a warrior to think about horses: a good and a bad. The warrior of old regarded his horse as an indispensable means of carrying him when he was clad in heavy armor with banner and all his war gear, which he could never have done on his two feet alone. And if his horse was wounded or even killed in battle, though it was only an animal he felt great compassion for it and took good care of it and saw that it was always well fed. But these days people buy a faulty mount at a low price and correct his defects, or they know how to pick out a country-bred colt and train him, so that they can sell at a good profit to somebody who takes a liking to him. This is the inward nature of a vet or a dishonest horse trader, but a very poor standard for a connoisseur of horse flesh.

軍法戰法

武士たらむものは。假令小身たり共。然るべき武者師を擇びて。兵法の傳授を致し。軍法戰法の奧秘に至るまで。委細に覺悟仕り罷在べき事に候。小身武士の軍法だて。不相應に思はるゝなど。申す者も有之候へ共。それは大きなる不吟味と可申候。子細を申すに。古今國郡の守護と仰がれ。良將の名を得玉ふ人々の中には。微賤孤獨より起りて。大業を立玉へる方々。いか程も有之候。然れば今とても。小身より仕出て立身を遂。一方の將共罷成事の有間數に非ず候。其上兵學を學び候へば。元來賢き者は益賢くなり。少々鈍き生れ付の者も。左のみ鈍なる事を申さぬ程には罷成物にて候。然れば。武士は必ず兵學を仕るべき事に候。

The Military Arts

One who is a samurai, even though only a small retainer, certainly should find himself a suitable instructor and study the traditional military arts so that he knows everything there is to be known about them. Some may say that this is not necessary for a small samurai, but I consider that to be a shallow view. In all ages many warriors have risen from quite humble positions to make a name as great generals and become lords of districts or provinces. Even now I do not think it impossible for a small vassal to become a commander of an army. In addition, study of the military arts will make one who is naturally clever more so and one who is born somewhat dull quite a bit less so. Therefore, all samurai certainly should apply themselves to it.

然りといへ共。兵法の修行を悪く仕り損ひ候へば。功者づき候程
我が智に高ぶり。寄障る人を見こなし。實理にもあらぬ。高上なる
理窟だてを申して。若輩の耳を誤らせ。氣立を傷ひ。口には正義正
法に似たる。分外の言葉を吐候へ共。心根は大に貪り。立にも居る
にも利害を謀り。次第に人柄悪く成り。武士の意地合までも取失
ふ者有之候。是兵學修行の中半なるに付ての過失に候。迚も兵を
學ぶとならば。此半途に足を止めず。如何にもして奥旨に至り。頓
て元の愚に立歸り。安住致すまでに。修行仕度事に候。然れ共。我
人兵學の半途に日を送り。奥義に至る事叶はず候ゆへ。本の愚に
立歸るべき方角を取失ひ狼狽罷在候は。心外の至りに候。爰に愚
に歸ると申すは。いまだ兵の道を學ばざる以前の心のごとくにと申
事に候。總じて味噌の味噌くさきと。兵法者の兵法くさきとに出會
候ては。鼻向もならざる物のよし。古來より申傳へ候。初心の武士
心得のため仍如件。

But a bad use can be made of this study to get a swelled head and disparage one's colleagues by a lot of high-flown but incorrect arguments that only mislead the young and crush their spirit. This kind of samurai utters a wordy discourse that may sound correct and proper, but actually he is only trying to impress others and thinking of his own advantage. The result is the deterioration of his character and the loss of the real samurai spirit. This is a fault arising from a superficial study of the subject. Those who begin it should never be satisfied to go only halfway, but should persevere until they understand all its secrets and only then return to their former simplicity and live a quiet life. But if people spend a lot of time in this study and yet prove unable to master it, they may not be able to regain their former simple condition, but instead may lapse into a confused state that is sad indeed. And by their former simplicity or ignorance I mean their mental capacity before they began to study the military arts. There is an old saying that bean sauce that smells of bean sauce is no good, and so it is with the military pedants.

治家

武士たらむもの。我が妻女の身の上に於て。心に叶はざる義有之候はゞ。事の道理をいひ分けて。よく合點致す樣に申し教へ。少々の義ならば思ひ免し。堪忍仕りて差置尤に候。然れ共元來心だて惡く。畢竟用に立間敷と存ずる程ならば。一向に暇を遣はし。親のもとへ送り返すは格別の義に候。

左ながら左樣にも致さず我が女房と定め。奧樣かみ樣と人にも言せて指置者へ對し。高聲を揚げ。種々の惡口雜言に及ぶは。市町の裏屋脊戸屋の。傭夫役丁の風情は格別。既に一騎役をも勤むる武士の所行には。決して有まじき義に候。

況や腰刀などをひねくり廻し。或は握り拳の一つもあて候類ひは。言語道斷の事にて臆病武士の仕業に候。子細を申すに武士の娘に生れ。人の女房と成程の年齡にて。男子の義ならば。人に拳をあてられては。中々こらへぬ筈なれども。女性の淺ましさに。是非なく涙を流して。堪忍をば仕るにて候。

總じて我に手向ひのならぬ相手と見懸て。理不盡の仕形に及ぶ義をば。猛き武士は決して致さぬものに候。猛き武士の嫌てせぬ事を。好みて致すものをさして。臆病者とは申にて候。初心の武士心得のため仍如件。

Household Management

If a samurai finds that his wife does not please him, he should argue with her and warn her gently. In small matters, he should be indulgent and patient with her. But if her disposition is consistently bad and he sees no further use in their staying together, he may, under these exceptional circumstances, divorce her and send her home to her parents.

But if he decides to keep her as his wife, and people start to address her with respectful titles like *okusama* and *kamisana,* then he may not shout at her and revile her in abusive language. Such behavior is suitable only to the mercenaries and common laborers who dwell in the back streets of the business quarter. It does not befit a samurai, who should act like a cavalier.

It is also unseemly for a samurai to lay hand on his sword or menace his wife with a clenched fist. These are outrageous acts that only a cowardly samurai would think of doing. A girl born in a warrior house and of marriageable age, if she were a man, would never for a moment tolerate being threatened with anyone's sword or fist. It is only because she was born a woman that she has to shed tears and put up with it.

To act like a bully toward someone weaker than himself is something a brave samurai never does. He who likes and does those things that a brave man hates and avoids is rightly described as a coward.

親族

世間において。我が兄の子をも。弟の子をも甥と申。又我が姉妹の
他へ嫁して設けたる子をも。同じく甥と名付て。何れも替る事なし
と心得罷在るは。百姓町人の上の事にて。武士は格別の様子有
之事に候。たとへば其家の嫡子たる兄の持たる子は。甥ながらも
我が親兄の跡式をふまひ。總領家と申すにて候へば。たとひ甥の
代となりても。親兄を敬ひたる如く馳走致す事に候。全く其甥に對
しての義にては無之。偏に家元の先祖を敬ふ道理にて候。

其二男三男。幷に我が弟の持たる子供へ對し候ては。世間體の伯
父甥の交りにて事濟み候。姉妹の持たる子共の義も。甥には候へ
共。是は他姓を禀たる義に候へば。其心得を以て。常の言葉づか
ひ。書状の文言などにも。隔意を用ひ尤に候。

Relatives

Farmers and shopkeepers usually call the children of both elder and younger brothers nephews, as they do those of married sisters, and treat them in the same way. But among samurai it is different. For instance, the son of an elder brother who is heir to a samurai's estate, since he is a nephew, will carry on the elder brother's house and so has legal rights as the heir presumptive. He is regarded as an elder brother and treated with the respect due him. This is not the ordinary treatment of a nephew, but rather the treatment of one who represents the ancestral founder of the family.

As for the second and third sons of that elder brother, it is enough that they be treated as ordinary nephews, as would be the sons of younger brothers. Sisters' male children are also nephews, but since they have outside relationships it is well to communicate normally with them, in both speech and writing, and to keep them at some distance.

甥弟又は。我子たりといふ共。他の家へ養子に遣し候ては。其心得あるべき事に候。たとひ内證の出合。參會の刻の言葉づかひなどは。いかんも候へ。他所他門のつき合に於ては。隔意の挨拶尤に候。他人の子に致したる後も。猶我が子我が弟のごとく。介抱だてを致すべき所存ならば。本より手前にさし置たるがよきにと。養父方の諸親類。向の家頼の下墨もなくては不叶候。但し養父方において。埒と致したる親類とても無之。家の締りもなく。相續なりがたき様子に付ては。實子實弟のあいさつなれば。見放しがたくて。餘儀なく世話に致すなどは。左もあるべき義に候。

次に我が娘を他へ嫁せしめ。男子産れて後。其聟相果。幼少の外孫家督に備はり。其跡式の義に付。聟の方の親類縁者と。立合相談の義など有之においては。十の物ならば。八つ九つまでも。聟の方の諸親類の取捌に致させて。指置申す心得肝要に候。但し其聟存生の時より。勝手不如意なる跡式などにて。諸親類の厄介とも罷成次第ならば。畢竟我が娘の難義をも。見届け遣はす道理にも有之候へば。彼是と世話にも不致しては不叶候。

其聟の果たる跡に。何の事欠る義も無之か。又は少しにてもたくはひなども有之ならば。猶以て舅方より手ざしは致さぬ筈の義に候。其孫とてもいまだ幼少なるに。我が娘と相談を以ての後見。一圓其意を得ぬと。他人の批判も憚るべき事に候。

If nephews and younger brothers and even one's own children are sent out as adopted children, they must be treated as such. Whether one meets them in private or speaks with them at some family meeting, greetings and salutations should be of a formal and distant nature, as with those of outside houses and families as opposed to near relatives. After they have gone to another house, if you continue to treat them as a son or younger brother, it will look as though you would have preferred to keep them at home. The adoptive father and the other family will regard that attitude as a snub. Yet that adoptive father is certainly not a relative, and if there should be disorder in his house and it proves to be difficult to decide who will inherit the estate, then it may be proper to treat a son or younger brother as such and to help them and not turn away from them.

And when you marry your daughter into another family, if she bears a son and then the husband dies so that the small grandson is left as the heir, you will have to negotiate with the relations and connections of this son-in-law to settle the estate. In this matter it is essential that, out of ten points of dispute, for instance, you leave eight or nine to be decided by them. But even if your daughter's husband remains alive, if his family is badly off and becomes a burden on the relatives, you can hardly hold yourself back from doing something to assist your daughter when in difficulties. In that case it is proper for a samurai to give some help.

But if your daughter's husband has died, and their family resources are sufficient, or they have some savings, it is not proper for a samurai to get involved. Even a discussion with your own daughter about the guardianship of your minor grandson becomes subject to criticism unless you have an agreement acceptable to all.

扨又一家の總領筋。或は先祖の主筋。旗頭など申す人の家衰へ。世に落ぶれて。見る影もなく成果たるを。少しも疎略致さず。むかしの筋目を立て。折々の心寄せをも仕るは。武士の本意に候。襟元足元にばかり目を付け。盛なると見ては。敬ふまじきをも敬まひ。衰へたると見ては。賤しむまじきをも賤しむは。悉皆百姓町人の意地合にして。武士の正義にあらず候。初心の武士心得のため仍

如件。

Moreover, even though a family of your own direct family line, or of the head of other branches of the ancestral line, or of standard bearers is in decline, or has lost its status in the eyes of the world and become a mere shadow of what it once was, a samurai will continue to treat its members politely as he always has and give them every consideration. This is his basic position. It is the mentality of peasants and merchants to judge a person by his outward appearance and social standing, respecting him when he is successful and looking down on him when he has fallen on hard times. This is not the upright moral conduct of a samurai.

儉嗇

奉公仕る武士は。大身小身に限らず。常に儉約を用ひて。隨分勝
手をすり切不申分別尤に候。但し知行高を取武士の義は。たとひ
一度勝手をすり切候ても。早く思案を致しかへて。爰をつめ彼所を
ちゞめ。諸事に氣を付て簡畧をさへ致候得ば。程なく勝手を取直
し申義も罷成候は。身上に餘計あるを以ての義に候。小身にて大
身の眞似を致し。無用の義に物を入れ。勝手を仕損じ候ては。身
上の餘計無之に付。萬事跡ひけになり。何程簡略致し候ても補ひ
兼。後々は跡へも先へも行兼る。大すり切と罷成るは必定に候。人
々勝手に成るぞ成らぬぞと申すは内證の義にて。奉公を致す身に
は。傍輩一列の格合有之。止事を得ざる物入もなくては叶はず。左
様の刻爲方なければ。種々の才覺手段に及び。云まじき事をもい
ひ。仕間敷事をも仕りて。生れも付ざる不律義もの。大はつ者の名
取を仕るも。畢竟不勝手より起る過失に候。

Thrift

Whether great or small, samurai who are in service to a feudal lord must always practice thrift and do so wisely in such a way that they do not run up a deficit in their own household expenditures. Samurai with a large income, if they find they are living beyond their means, can quickly make a change in their affairs. By making a saving here and cutting an expense there, they can soon recover their solvency because they will have a bit of surplus. But if a small retainer tries to live like a great vassal, spends unnecessary amounts, and then gets into difficulties, he cannot recover because he has nothing to fall back on. However much he tries to scrimp and save, he only becomes more involved until at last he comes to complete ruin. But because people's domestic affairs are a private matter, and one who is in service must do as his colleagues do and incur certain necessary expenses, he will be forced to try every possible trick and device. He will even say what should not be said, and do what should not be done, since financial difficulty induces even those with a high reputation to do dishonest things that are otherwise alien to them.

爰を以て前かたより其覺悟を定め。身上相應の暮しを仕り。少し
なり共無益の義には。物を入ぬ分別を仕り。是非致さずしては叶
はざる事ばかりに物を入る。是を儉約の道と申候。但此儉約に付
て一つの心得有之候。いかんとなれば。儉約儉約とばかり申て。物
の費をいとひ。内證をつめて簡略專らなる時は。程なく勝手を持直
し。其初め持つけぬ金銀を持てば。持つほど多くなるを悦び。耗を
悲しむむさき心と成り。

後々は爲べき事をもせず。致さで叶はぬ事をも致さぬ。義理知らず
となり。兎にも角にも金銀を蓄ふる分別の外無之。之を名付て吝
嗇と申候。百姓町人の上はいかんも候へ。武士の吝嗇と申すは。
三寶の棄物とやらんにて。大きに嫌ひ申義に候。其子細は。世に多
き金銀をさへ。義理にかへて。遣ふ事をいやがり候心からは。まし
てや外に二つとなき一命を惜し氣もなく捨る義は。決して無之道
理に候。されば社吝嗇は。臆病の唐名なりと。古き人の申置候事
に候。初心の武士心得のため仍如件。

Thus, one must firmly resolve to live only according to one's means and take great care not to indulge in any useless expenses, spending money only on what is necessary. This is what is called the Way of Economy. But one thing must be noted: To do nothing but talk about economizing, and to hate to spend anything, saving and skimming everywhere and being delighted when you can add one coin to another by some tightfisted trick, is to become devoted to dirty money.

A man who in this way eventually loses all sense of decency will do what ought not to be done and will leave undone what should be done. People like that lose all instincts except that of hoarding and what they practice is miserliness, not thrift. However it may be with peasants and merchants, stinginess in a samurai is as much to be despised as throwing away the Three Sacred Treasures. For if he puts all the money there is before duty, and spends it grudgingly, how much more will he grudge throwing away his far more precious life? That is why in China the ancients regarded extreme frugality as being the same as cowardice.

家作

奉公仕る武士。家作仕るにおいては。表向の門長屋。玄關の見入。座敷の體などは。身上相應に暉麗に仕るも尤の義に候。子細は。何れの城下に於ても。外曲輪の邊までは。他所他國の者も入來り。見る事も有之候に。諸士の家居宜しければ。家中も落付て覺ゆるなれば。主君の御爲にも。少しは宜敷道理も有之かにて候。其外奥向。妻子など指置候處は。雨さへ漏ずば。いか樣に見苦しくても堪忍仕り。成べき程は。家普請に物を入ざる樣にと覺悟尤に候。

House Construction

It is fitting that a samurai who is in service should have his outer gate and guardhouse, his porch and entrance as well as his reception room, be as fine as his income allows. In all castle towns, people from elsewhere come in as far as the outer moats to take a look around, and if the samurai's residence looks pleasing on the outside and seems quiet and dignified on the inside, it will reflect well both on his lord and on himself. But otherwise the inner parts of the house where the samurai's wife and family live should be considered adequate, even if they appear unsightly, so long as they keep the rain out. For it is most important that one should spend as little as possible on repairs or renovations.

子細を申すに。亂世には城主たる大名方にも。常に籠城の心懸お
はしますを以て。二三の丸に罷在士屋敷は。家を低く。梁間をつめ
て。普請を手輕くとの制を定めらるゝ事に候。ましてや外曲輪に住
居仕る士共の家宅は。變に臨みては。悉く自燒致して取拂ふ事な
れば。末を兼たる家作とては。可仕様も無之候。去るに依て。作事
の至て輕きをば。寢小屋普請の様なりとは申にて候。

爰を以て存ずる時は。たとひ治世の今とても。武士道を磨く士は。
居屋敷の家作に種々の物數寄を盡し。常住の思ひをなすは。有之
間敷事に候。其上火災などに逢たる時は。早速似合の小屋掛不
仕ては叶はず候に。左様の勘辨もなく。分限に過たる普請に物を
入れ。それを借金の高に結びて嬉しがり候は。至極の不物數寄と
より外には。可申様も無之候。初心の武士心得のため仍如件。

In this unsettled world, even the lord of a castle must always bear in mind the possibility of a siege, and therefore the samurai residences within the second and third districts must be kept low and of shallow depth and inexpensive to build. By contrast, those retainers who live in the outer zone, who may have to burn their houses to the ground in time of emergency, should refrain from building anything too permanent. Their dwelling should, in fact, be of the lightest possible construction, barely more than a shed to sleep in.

Realizing all this, even though just now we are living in a time of peace, a samurai who wishes to keep his Bushido untarnished will not think of his house as a permanent residence, nor will he lavish any care on elaborate decorations. If the house catches fire, he will have to put up a suitable shelter again in a hurry. Anyone who fails to think ahead, but instead spends too much money on building, and perhaps even runs up a heavy debt for fancy furnishings, can only be considered to lack a sense of the fitness of things.

武備

奉公を勤る武士は。分限相應に。武具兵具を貯へずしては不叶
候。就中其家々の軍法有之。兼々主君より定め置るゝ家中一同の
番指物。同じく面々の出子。或は冑の前立。鎗印。袖印。小荷駄印
など申す合印に於ては。油斷なく支度尤に候。其期に臨み俄に支
度候ては。日比の油斷も顯はれ。人の下墨も如何に候。合印を疎
略に致して。味方討に逢たる者は。討れ損たるべき旨。武家の古法
に相見え候。然れば油斷可仕樣とては無之候。

たとへば我召仕のものに。人を斬る用が無きとて。刀脇指の身を木
竹に致し。尻をからくる用が無きとて。肌帶をかゝずして罷在樣な
る。不心掛者有之ば。其通りに致しては指置がたき道理に候。況
や一騎前を勤る武士。似合の祿を受て居ながら軍役の勤めの。成
るぞ成らぬぞといふ了簡もなく。如何に靜謐の時代なればとて。持
ずして叶はざる。武具兵具の用意に不足するは。右に申す刀脇差
の身に木竹を用ひ。下帶をかゝぬ若黨仲間には。百双倍も優りた
る不心掛者と可申候。然れば深く恥恐れて。武備の心掛油斷有べ
からず。是に付心得有之候。

Weapons

Every samurai who is in service to a lord must have a supply of weapons suitable to his means. Each feudal house has its military regulations, so the proper banners and flags and helmet insignia, spear mounts, sleeve crests, and marks on the pack animals as ordered by the lord must be carefully provided in a uniform manner. If any have to be improvised in haste, it will be an obvious sign of carelessness and will provoke contempt. Not unknown in military history are men who by neglect of their insignia have been attacked by their own side and killed and suffered loss. Therefore precautions must always be taken in such matters.

Some samurai may think that their servants are not likely to have to cut anybody down and so may replace their sword-blades with wood or bamboo, and fail to provide them with a loincloth because they think they will not need to cinch up their clothes, and will find themselves in difficulty because of their lack of foresight. And a samurai who is a cavalier receiving a considerable salary and who does not know when he may have to take the field, however peaceful the time may seem to be, is a hundred percent more blameworthy if he does not provide himself with the proper weapons than the young serving man with a wooden sword or no loincloth. So out of fear of being publicly shamed he must equip himself properly. Here is a piece of advice on the subject:

小身の武士。着料の具足新たに威し立可申とならば。譬ば黄金三
枚を以て。一領の具足を調る覺悟ならば。其内三分二を甲冑の代
に心當。残る金子にては。肌着。股引。上着。下袴。上帶。下帶。陣
羽織。鞭。扇。或は腰桶。腰苞。面桶。打懸。水筒。水飲などまでも。
一騎前の諸色不足なく。具足と一同に。支度仕る義肝要に候。扨
又其身年若く。力量勝れたり共。鐵厚なる重具足。大差物。大立物
などをば遠慮尤に候。子細を申すに。若盛りの力量に合せて。調置
たる具足は。年寄候ての用に不立。其上如何に年若く候ても。陣中
に於て病氣か。又手疵など負ひては。假令薄鐵の具足たり共。肩
を引し。苦勞になるは定り事に候。爰を以て重具足を無用とは申す
にて候。次に大指物大立物の義も。若き時分より。陣毎に是を用
ひ。世間の人に見知られたる上にては。其身年寄苦勞になればと
て。指止がたきものに候。初心の武士心得のため仍如件。

When a small retainer wishes to outfit himself and has, let us say, three pieces of gold to buy a suit of armor, the best thing he can do will be to spend two-thirds of it on the body armor and helmet. This will leave the remainder to provide all the other items he will need, such as underclothes, breeches, coat, under-*hakama*, upper sash, great-coat to wear over his armor, whip, fan, wallet, cloak, water-bottle, cup, and so forth. In this way he will have every accessory he needs, as well as his suit of armor. And even though he may be young and wonderfully strong, it is better for him to avoid heavy suits of thick iron armor and hefty banners and flags. For, while they may be tolerable while he is youthful and vigorous, as he grows older they will become too much for him. Even a young man may fall ill or be wounded, and then the lightest iron armor will be a heavy burden and an obstacle. If a young man acquires a reputation for the weight of his banners and flags, he will find it hard to give them up when he grows older and becomes less able to carry them.

從僕着具

小身なる武士は。不慮の變有之刻も。人多く召連候義無之ゆゑ。
鎗壹本より外には。持する義成らず候。もし其鎗折損じ候に於て
は。持鎗に事を欠は定り事に候。去るに依て。兼て袋鎗の身を支
度仕り。柄には竹を仕すげ候てなり共。當用の間に合せ候心掛尤
に候。

且又少々疵有之候ても。作り丈夫にして。寸の延たる刀を用意し
て。下人共にさゝせ。若黨には胴丸鉢鐵。小者中間には胸懸鉢卷。
又は鐵笠など。輕き身の圍ひを致して取らせ候は。小身武士の心
掛共可申候。扨又太刀打の勝負を遂るには。具足冑の上といふ見
合も無之候得ば。大方は刀を打折。指替に事を欠事も無くては不
叶候。去るに依て。我が指替の刀を若黨にさゝせ。若黨の刀を草
履取。又は馬の口取などにさゝせて召連尤に候。初心の武士心得
のため仍如件。

On the Equipment of Servants

A small retainer, even on singular occasions, should not venture out with many servants, and so need not have more than one spear. If that one gets damaged, he will be without a spear to be carried before him. So he should keep an extra spear-blade, which can be fitted with a bamboo shaft and used in the meantime, for it is important that he should have something right now.

And if his spear is only slightly damaged, he can provide a rather long, strongly mounted sword and let his attendants carry that. The young squires may use a *domaru* armor with an iron helmet, and the underservants and attendants a *munekake* with only a cloth around their head or an iron hat, for a small retainer should take care to arm his men lightly. And if you should be caught up in a bout of fencing, in which armor and helmet are used, your sword will probably get its edge nicked and you will need to replace it with another. Then the old one can be used by the young squire and later be passed on to the sandal-bearer or the horse-tender.

武士

總じて武士と申すものは。世の亂賊を誅し三民の輩に。安堵の思
ひをなさしむべき爲の役人に候へば。たとひ小身たり共。武士と呼
るゝ身としては。三民の輩に對して。無理非道の仕形とては。仕間
敷道理に候處。農人へは無體なる收納を申懸。其上に種々の過役
を充て取潰し。職人には物をあつらへて。其作料手間代をも遣ら
ず。町人商人の手前よりは物を調へて。其代物を無沙汰に致し。或
は金銀を借りても。横に寝て借取に仕るは。大不義と可申候。

爰を能々勘辨致し。領知の百姓をば勞はり。諸職人をもたふさぬ
様に仕り。町人商人の手前に。是まで有之買掛り借金等も。たとひ
一度にこそは返濟不罷成候共。連々を以て少しづゝも是を遣はし。
損をさせ。迷惑を致させぬ様にと。心入有べき事に候。盜賊を戒む
る役人たる武士として。盜賊の眞似を仕るべき様とては無之事に
候。初心の武士心得のため仍如件。

Samurai

Because samurai are officials whose business it is to destroy rebels and unruly elements and bring peace and security to the farmers, merchants, and artisans, even the least of those who bear this title must never commit any violence or injustice against these three classes. That is to say, he must not demand any more revenue than is customary from the farmers or wear them out by forced service. He must not order goods from artisans and then forget to pay them. Neither must he send for things from townspeople and shopkeepers and keep them waiting for their money. It is also most incorrect to lend them money and charge high interest on it as a mere silent partner.

One should always be considerate to these people, sympathetic to the farmers on one's estates, and careful that the artisans are not ruined by debt. And though you might not be able to settle the debts you may have incurred in transactions with townspeople and shopkeepers all at once, you certainly ought to pay a portion from time to time so as not to cause these classes loss and distress. For samurai whose duty it is to punish robbers and thieves must not imitate their criminal ways.

廉恥

五六十年以前までは。諸浪人の身上をかせぎ候言葉に。乗替の
壹疋も繋ぎ申す程に無之てはと申すは。知行五百石以上ならばと
申義に候。責て痩馬壹疋も繋ぎ申す様にといふは。三百石ほどな
らばと。云ぬ計りの口上に候。錆鎗の壹本も持せ候様にと申すは。
百石にても。知行取といふ名に。望を懸たる言葉に候。

其時代までは武士の古風殘り。我が口より何百石などゝ。員數を
定めては申出間敷との。意地より出たる言葉に候。鷹は飢ても穗を
啄ず。武士は喰ねど高楊枝など申すも。其時代の世話にて。年若き
人は。勝手損徳の話。物の直段などをば口にいはず。女色の話を
聞ては。赤面する様に候ひき。士たらむものは。及ばぬまでも。古風
の武士偏義を。慕ひ學び度事にて候。たとひ鼻は曲りても。息さへ
出ればよきといふ意地合に罷成候ては。是非に及ばず候。初心の
武士心得のため仍如件。

Sense of Shame

Fifty or sixty years ago, when speaking of employment, lordless samurai would say that a man could scarcely keep a spare horse with an income of something over five hundred *koku*, or that one could barely afford to keep a half-starved animal if he had about three hundred. Similarly, if they heard about a vacant position with an income of a hundred, they would describe it as allowing a man to own only one rusty spear.

For up until then the ancient style of the samurai still survived, and it was not their habit to mention figures and say that anyone had so many *koku* of income. Instead, they used these expressions: "A hawk may be starving but he won't touch corn," and "The samurai may have eaten nothing, but he still uses his toothpick." Sayings such as these illustrate this sentiment. Young people of that day never spoke of profit or loss or mentioned the price of anything. They would even blush if they heard any talk about love affairs. And though all samurai may not be able to attain these ancient ideals, I think all ought to admire and study them. We should think of it this way: "Though a man's nose be crooked, if he can breathe through it, then all is well."

擇友

奉公仕る武士は。多き傍輩の中にても。勇氣有りて義理を正す事を好み。智惠才覺有りて口をきく武士とは。日比入魂致し。内外心安く申合する義尤に候。右様の武士は。左のみ澤山には無之ものに候へば。壹人にても。自餘の友達幾人にも懸合ひ。何事ぞ有之時は。大きに便りと罷成物にて候。總じて武士の友達をえらぶ事なく。彼とも是とも狎れ睦び。飲食の交りを致し。出入を繁く仕るは宜しからず候。

子細を申すに。武士の入魂を仕るは。互ひの心根をも見届け。見とゞけられてこそ。念比には可罷成を。當分出會て面白きぞ。合口なるぞと申す迄にて。心易だてを仕り。武士の出會の様にも無之。不禮不作法のみを盡し。手足をもたせあひて。小歌淨瑠璃にて夜を明し。うぬがわがと挨拶よきかと思へば。假初の事を申しつのりて。不通義絶を致し。誰有りて中をなほす者の無きにも。頓て又中をなほり候など。一つとして踏詰たる意地の無之は。貌は武士にても。心は夫人足に等しき様子にて。恥愼しむべき事に候。初心の武士心得のため仍如件。

Choice of Friends

It is most important that a samurai in service should associate with and make friends of only those among his colleagues who are valiant, dutiful, wise, and influential. But because men of this kind are not numerous, he may find only one among all his friends on whom he can thoroughly rely in time of need. Generally speaking, it is not desirable for a samurai to make any intimate friend of whom he is especially fond and with whom he prefers to eat and drink and chase around.

For if he discovers a kindred spirit and makes a great friend of him, thinking he will be an amusing and convivial companion, the two may come to behave in a manner inappropriate for their class. They may treat each other with no ceremony or reserve, sprawling up against each other, spending their evenings bawling songs and *joruri* ballads, or using too-familiar terms of address. They may seem best friends at one moment, and then, by insisting on some small thing, breaking up and not on speaking terms the next. Then they may just as quickly patch up their friendship without even asking someone's help as reconciler, as is the custom. Such unpardonable lack of dignity shows that, though some may look like samurai on the outside, their minds are those of ditch diggers.

交誼

武士たらむものゝ。頼母しき意地有之と申すは。武道の正義に候。
然りといへ共。譯もなく頼母しだてを致し。懸も構はぬ所へもさし
出。我が苦勞に成まじき事をも。荷なひ取持候をば。さし出者共申
し。又は物に懸りなどゝも沙汰仕り。大きに宜しからず候。是は少し
構ひてもと存ずる事なりとも。人が頼まぬ事ならば。かまわぬ程好
事は無之候。子細を申すに。小事はいふに及ばず。たとひいか様の
むづかしき事たり共。武士の上に於て。既に頼むぞ頼まるゝぞと申
すに至り候ては。我が身に引懸。苦勞に不仕しては不叶候。事の首
尾によりては。主君親兄弟の爲にさへ。無差と捨ぬ一命をも。是非
なく相果す儀も有まじきに非ず。爰を以て譯もなき頼母しだてを。
無用とは申にて候。

古き武士は。人に物を頼まれ候へば。成る筋。成らぬ筋を勘辨仕
りて。成まじきと存ずる事をば。最初より請負不申。可成筋の義と
存ずる義も。篤と思案致して後。其義を受負申すに付。既に受負候
ほどの義は相調ひ。首尾不合の義とては無之物にて候。去るに依
て。人も埒明哉と申して。譽事にも仕るにて候。然るに其考なしに。
人が物をさへ頼めば。心易く受負。首尾不合なれども。それを何共
不存候時は。不埒者といふ名取を仕り候。

Friendship

Reliability is one of the qualities that the Way of the Warrior requires of a samurai. Yet it is not at all desirable that he should offer assistance for no special reason, thrust himself forward in things that do not matter, or take on obligations in affairs that do not concern him, merely for the sake of doing so or of giving his advice. Even in things that do concern him even slightly, it is much better to stand aloof unless someone asks him to intervene. If a samurai becomes implicated in even small questions, let alone more complicated ones, he may become so entangled that he cannot withdraw without risking his precious life, which should be at the disposal only of his lord or his parents. Therefore, I say that he should not perform favors without good cause.

If the samurai of former days was asked to do a service, he would think about whether it was one that could be granted or not; if the latter, he would decline at once. If he did entertain the request, he would undertake it only after careful thought, so that he was fully prepared to deal with it and the entire affair could be settled soon. As a result, the suppliant's difficulties were resolved and the benefactor samurai gained great praise. If, on the other hand, without such reflection someone takes on certain responsibilities, he will be unable to carry them through properly and will thereby gain a reputation for having no principles.

扨又人に我が思ひ寄を申し。或は異見を加へ候も。勘辨あるべき
事にて候。子細を申すに。人の親師匠。兄伯父などの身にて。子や
弟子や。甥弟へ對しては。たとひいか様の思ひ寄を申過し候ても。
苦しかるまじく候へ共。それさへ武士の口より物を申出すは。遠慮
勘辨なくては不叶候。況や友傍輩へ對し候ては。猶更遠慮尤に
候。扨又人より打わりて。相談を致し懸る義有之節。我等も了簡に
及ばずと云て。一向相談を斷り候は格別の義に候。既に其相談相
手と罷成より初めては。たとひ其人の心に叶はず。氣に入らぬ事な
りとも。少しも遠慮なく道理をせめて。我が存寄の一とほりを殘ら
ず申述るは。一段頼母しき意地に候。

然るを心弱くて。ケ様に申したらんには。若も心に障るべきか。氣に
當るべきかなど。下手遠慮を致して。事の道理に背き。筋目にあら
ざる義を。尤左様にも可然など。間に合なる相談に及び。其人に云
まじき事をいはせ。或は仕形の負を取らせなど致して。後日人々の
誹嘲りに逢せ候は。相談相手に頼まれたる甲斐もなき仕合に候。
或は我を人がましく思ひて。相談を致すに付て。理の當る所を以
て。相談に及ぶ義を不用して。己が心任せに致し。事を仕損ずる様
なる無分別ものならば。向後入魂仕間敷事に候。初心の武士心得
のため仍如件。

Then again, giving one's advice or opinion should be done only after much thought. For though parents, teachers, elder brothers, uncles, and so on may give unsuitable advice to their children, pupils, and nephews without harming them much, everything that comes out of a samurai's mouth must be considered and guarded. Particularly to his friends and colleagues must he use words most carefully. And when he is singled out and asked to take part in a discussion he may, of course, say that he has no views on the subject and refuse to talk about it. But if he does become a party to the discussion, he will prove most helpful by stating exactly what he thinks, clearly and succinctly, without hesitation and with no regard for the others' disapproval or resentment.

For if, out of weakness, he fears opposing people or offending them and so betrays an awkward indecision, turns aside from what is just, and agrees with what is not reasonable, and, to avoid a squabble, allows improper things to be said and burdens to be laid on others, then he will come to be thought of as a worthless advisor and may even be despised and vilified for it. Again, if anyone is so stupid as to think himself too lofty a person to take part in an important discussion, arguing that there is no need to consult the others but instead wishing to decide everything according to his own preferences, and so making a mess of things, he will likely find himself not very popular among his fellows.

絶交

奉公仕る武士。傍輩の中に何ぞ子細有て。不通義絶のものも可有之候。然るに主君の仰を以て。其の者と同役に罷成候節は。早速其者の方へ罷越。我等義今度貴殿と同役に仰付られ御請に及び候。其許とは日比義絶の義に候得共。既に同役と仰付られ候上は。向後互ひに隔意なく申合せ。御用の相滞り不申候様に無之てはと存ずる事に候。其許は當役に於て先輩の義にも候へば。諸事御指南頼入存候。但明日にも貴殿我等の内他役に轉じ。同僚を離れ候はゞ。又義絶に及び可申候。それまでの義は。隔意なく申合せ候外無之段申理り。互ひに心を合せて相勤るは。武士の正義に候。況や日比何の子細無之傍輩と。同役の義ならば。尚更隔意なく申合せずしては叶はず候。

然るをやゝもすれば權を爭ひ。或は新役にて諸事不案内なるには。氣をつけ心を添て。首尾好勤めさせべきといふ。おとなしき心はなく。仕落有之を見ては嬉しがり申すなどは。むさきともきたなきとも。兎角の批判に及ばず候。左樣なる心立の武士は。自然の變に臨みては。必定奪ひ首。味方討等。卑怯なる働きをも仕兼ず候。尤恥愼しむべき事に候。初心の武士心得のため仍如件。

Breaking Off Relations

A samurai who is in service may well have among his acquaintances or comrades one with whom, for some reason, he does not wish to associate. But if he is ordered by his lord to serve with such a person he should go to him at once and say, "I am commanded to serve with you, and though so far we have not been on speaking terms, as things are, I trust you will cooperate with me so that we can carry out our duties properly without any difficulties." And if the other is his senior in office, he will ask him to give him the benefit of his kind instruction. If he is transferred to some other position the very next day, then both of them should revert to their former terms, but meanwhile they must agree to work together cordially in carrying out their official duties, as is the correct conduct for a samurai. Between comrades who face no such obstacle there should always be the most hearty mutual cooperation when they find themselves serving together.

But those who constantly strive for power, who lack the kindness of heart to give assistance to those who are new to office and little acquainted with its details, or who even rejoice when such novices make mistakes, such men show a nasty, mean spirit and fully deserve to be sternly condemned. This is the sort of samurai who might play some dirty trick, like turning against his own side when he finds himself in an awkward situation. Anything of the kind is to be strictly avoided.

名譽

武士たらむものは。常に古き記録を披見致して。其身の覺悟を相極め尤に候。子細を申すに。世の人のもてはやし候。甲陽軍鑑。信長記。太閤記など申す書の中に。合戰の次第を記し置候にも。名譽の働を遂たる輩の義は。誰がし何某と其姓名を顯はし。此外討死都合何千何百と相記し有之候。右何千何百と申す人數の内には。大身の士いか程も可有之候得共。させる働も無之を以て。其名を書記すに及ばず候。小身にても。勝れたる武篇有之武士ばかりは擇拔て。姓名を書顯はしたる物にて候。右姓名も殘らぬ程の討死を致すも。又末世末代まで譽れを殘す討死を遂るも。敵に首を渡す時の苦痛に。替りとては無之道理に候。

爰を能々分別致し。迚も捨る身命ならば。諸手に勝れたる働を仕りて討死を遂。敵味方の耳目を驚かし。主君大將の御惜みにも預り。子孫永々の面目にも備へむと心懸るこそ。武士の本意にて候。然るに意地きたなくして。懸る時は人の後。退く時は人の先とばかり心を働かせ。或は敵城を攻る砌も。矢玉の劇しき所にては。傍輩を楯につき。其陰にかゞみ居り。遁れぬ運の矢には中りて伏倒れ。剩へ味方の踏草にまで成りて。犬死を仕り。大切の身命を失ひ候は。無念の至り。口惜しき次第にて。武士の不覺此上有るべからず候。此旨能々思量致し。朝思暮練の工夫あるべき事に候。初心の武士心得のため仍如件。

Reputations

One who is a samurai should always be reading the ancient records so that he may strengthen his character. Those works that are famous everywhere, such as the *Koyo Gunkan,* the *Nobunagaki,* and the *Taikoki,* give accounts of battles, with detailed descriptions and the names of those who fought gallantly as well as the numbers of those who fell. Among these latter might be many great vassals, even though in fact they were not conspicuous for their valor and thus their names were not recorded. Even among the small retainers, only those whose martial valor was preeminent have been selected for the honor rolls and their names inscribed for posterity. Yet both the fallen who left no name behind and those whose exploits are famous through the ages felt the same pain when the enemy cut their heads off.

So consider this well: Because every samurai must die, his aim should be to fall while performing some great deed of valor that will astonish friend and foe alike. His brave act will make his lord and commander regret his death, and in this way he will leave behind an illustrious name to the generations to come. Very different is the fate of the coward who is the last to charge and the first to retreat, and who, when attacking a stronghold, uses his comrades' bodies to shield himself against the enemy's arrows and spears. Struck by a chance arrow, he falls and dies a dog's death, and may even be trampled underfoot by his own side. This is the greatest disgrace for a samurai and should never be forgotten but pondered over earnestly, both day and night.

大口惡口

武士の上に大口ものと惡口ものと有之。相似たる樣にて。大きに違ふと心得るがよく候。子細を申すに。古き武士の中には。大口者の名を得たる士いか程も有之。既に公儀の御旗本においても。松平加賀右衛門。大久保彦左衛門など申たる人々は。隨分の大口きゝに候。其時代には諸國大名方の家々にも。五人三人づゝ。大口者の聞へある士の無は無之候。其大口者と申すは。何れも數度の武功手柄を顯し。武士道一通りに於ては。殘る所なしといへ共。時折節には偏情を張り。物の相談相手に成兼候所が。身上の抑へと成り。其身の高名譽れに合せては。知行も職役も不足なるより事起りて。わざくれ心と成り。相手を嫌はず。きれ口の言度まゝを申すといへども。主君を初め家老年寄も。其者共の義をば制外のごとく。見遁し聞逃し候故。いよいよ我儘つのり。遠慮會釋もなく。人の善惡を申散し。一生大口をきゝ死に仕る。是を昔の大口者と申候。其大口もの共は。腕に覺ありての大口に候。

今時の大口ものは。具足を一度肩に懸たる覺えもなくて。おのれが相口なる友傍輩と打寄ては。主君の御家の仕置の善惡。或は家老用人の難非をあげ。其外諸傍輩の噂までをも。腹一ぱいに申散し。おのれ等ばかり利發也と。存ずる樣なる空氣ものゝ義は。昔の大口者とは天地雲泥の違なれば。是を名付て惡口者共。亦は馬鹿口たゝき共可申候。初心の武士心得のため仍如件。

Braggarts and Slanderers

Though those who brag too much and those who speak slanderously may seem to be much alike, in fact they are quite different. In days gone by many samurai had a reputation of being braggarts—for example, Matsudaira Kagaemon and Okubo Hikozaemon, both officers of the shogun's guard. Indeed, in those days every daimyo was likely to have several samurai of this type. While such men had many great exploits to their credit and were in no way deficient in the Way of the Warrior, on occasion they could turn stubborn and thus be difficult parties in a conference. When they were hard-pressed in their living conditions and some incident arose from their having an income and office incompatible with their high reputation, they would become reckless and say whatever they pleased without any regard for who heard it. But their lord and the councilors and elders of their clan would overlook it or take no notice, so that they became more and more willful and would tell anyone what they thought of their good or bad points without reserve or apology. This they continued to do all their days. Such were the braggarts of old, men with a record of great deeds.

But today's braggarts are fellows who have never even put on a suit of mail, and who spend most of their time sitting with their friends and acquaintances discussing the defects of their lord's government, and pointing out the failings of the councilors and commissioners. They certainly do not hesitate to speak up about their own comrades' misdeeds, while at the same time emphasizing their own superiority. Such shallow men are a world apart from those brave braggarts of old, and should properly be called slanderers or just fools and show-offs.

旅行

奉公仕る武士旅行の道中に於て。小身者は乗懸馬にも乗らずして
は不叶候。然るに於ては。落馬の時の爲。刀脇差の鞘走らざる心
得を仕り。大小共にさし堅めて乗べき事に候。去りながら三尺手
拭などを以て。刀の柄を蒲團ばりに靉とゆひ付るは。有まじき事に
候。持鎗の鞘留を致すとて太き緒縄にて括り留るなども同然。一
分の不心懸と申のみにも無之。小荷駄印荷札の書付に。何某家來
と記しあれば。主人の家風までも。手淺き様に見ゆる物にて候。

Travel

When on a journey, a samurai in service, if he is only a small retainer, should ride with the baggage on a packhorse. In case he should fall off he must tie up his two swords together so that they do not slip from their scabbards. But he ought not tie up the hilt of the long sword into a thick bundle with a three-foot towel. Nor should he tie up the sheath of the spear with a thick rope to keep it on his body. He must not be the least careless about these things. If you put on your baggage some insignia or labels such as "Retainer of Lord So-and-so," it may appear somewhat disrespectful to his house.

扨又今時道中の習ひにて。馬郎共の相對を以て。馬をかふると申義有之候。向の乗人武士ならば。馬郎の申に任せ。馬より下るゝ躰を見届け候て後。此方も馬より下り可申候。子細は。馬郎共の言に任せて。此方は馬より下り立たるに。もし向の乗人。馬を替まじきと申す時は。是非替んといふ事もならず。然れば折角馬より下り候ても。又乗らずしては不叶との遠慮に候。

道中徒渡りの川にては。必ず所の川越を雇ひて。越行べき事に候。少しの費を厭ひ。或は水功者を恃みて自分越にいたし。川中にて馬を倒して。荷物を水に浸し。或は下人に怪我を致させ候は。大きなる不調法に候。

或は道のり近きとて。四日市のりを致し。又は粟津の船に乗る類ひは。無分別の至極に候。子細を申すに。天下の人の往還たる。桑名の船に乗て。風波の難に逢たるには。申譯も相立申候。いはれざる手廻しだてを仕りて。脇道を通り。事の間違ひ有之に於ては。一言の申開きも無之事に候。去るに依て古人の歌に

　ものゝふの　。
　矢橋のわたり。
　近くとも。
　いそがばまわれ。
　瀬田の長はし。

か様の心得は。道中の義のみに限らず。何事に付ても。此心持なくては不叶候。初心の武士心得のため仍如件。

And when, as is the custom on journeys nowadays, you get a horse direct from the horse-groom, if the previous rider is a samurai, you should wait to dismount yourself until he has dismounted at the ostler's bidding. The reason is that if you dismount at the groom's bidding and stand there, the other samurai will feel impelled to change his own mount even though he may not have had that intention. And if one has taken the trouble to get off a horse, he may feel embarrassment if he has to mount again.

In crossing rivers en route one should always engage a wading coolie. For if you grudge the expense or think you are an expert in the water, and cross without one and your horse falls and the luggage gets wet and perhaps a servant is injured, you will look most foolish.

Or again, with the idea of shortening the journey, if you ride at Yokkaichi or get on a boat at Awazu, you will be most shortsighted. If you go by the ordinary boat from Kuwana and then meet with rough weather, you have some excuse. But if you take a lot of trouble and go by a little-traveled side road and any mishap occurs, there is no excuse at all. So the old verse advises,

Does the warrior think
That the ford at Yabase
Is the nearer way?
He should know that the shortest road
Goes around by the Seta Bridge.

This principle of the longest way's being the shortest does not only apply to roads. It must be kept in mind in everything you do.

戒背語

主君を持奉公仕る武士は。諸傍輩の身の上の悪事を見聞ても。陰噂を仕間敷と。常々たしなみ肝要に候。如何となれば。我が身とても我知らず。いか様の致し損じ心得違ひ。有るべきも計られず。其上總じて家老年寄をはじめ諸役人の義は。主君の御目がねを以て。仰付らるゝ事にて候へば。其面々の義を悪しく申す時は。主君を誇り申すも同然の義に候。

又何ぞに付。其人を頼まずして叶はざる用事ある時は。機嫌を見合せ。手を束ね。膝を屈め。偏に頼み入存ずるなどゝも。いはねばならぬ事も有るまじきに非ず候。只今までは陰うしろに於て。誹り嘲りたる口を嗪めて。如何に用があればとて武士たる者の口より。申出されたる口上にては無之候。初心の武士心得のため仍如件。

Backbiting

A samurai who is in a lord's service must always take great care not to indulge in repeating any of the mean or spiteful things about his comrades that he may come to hear of or see. For a man cannot estimate by how much he may have unwittingly mistaken or misunderstood these things. Moreover, since the clan officials and particularly the councilors and senior officers are the spokesmen of the views of their lord, any criticism of them is a reflection on him.

Then again, you may one day have to approach them with some request. To consider their mood then, and to clasp your hands and bend your knees and humbly beg their favor, and suddenly to have to change your tone when moments before you were slandering someone behind his back, is the kind of thing that no samurai ought to bring himself to do, however important his business.

陳代

戦國の時代。合戦迫合の砌。よき働を致し討死仕るか。又は深手負て。其療養叶はず相果候士をば。主君大將も。別して不便に思召をもつて。たとひ當歳生れにてもあれ。男をさへ持候へば。跡式に於ては。相違なく被下置義に候。然れ共其子幼少にて。軍役の勤め不罷成に付。其親の弟など。浪人にて罷在候へば。當分其者に兄の遺跡を賜り。此者幼年の間は。後見を仕れと。主君より仰付らるゝ義有之。是を陣代と申候。

此陣代に古法有之候。其子細は。右の次第を以て。兄の遺跡を相續仕るからは。甥ながらも我が實子と存じ。眞實に不便を加へて養育仕るは。勿論の義に候。扨兄の跡式を受取候はゞ。武具馬具等は申すに及ばず。外々の雜具に至るまで。一所に集め。一家の内にて一兩輩も立合せて。委細に是を改め。悉く帳面に記し置義肝要に候。

War Substitute

In the civil war period when battles raged constantly, if a samurai was killed after a gallant fight or died of wounds received in it, his lord or commander would, out of regard for his services, allow his son, if he had one, however young, to inherit his position and gains of office. But if this son was only an infant he could not perform any military service, so his father's younger brother, if not in service, would inherit the position of his elder brother and be appointed by his lord as his guardian. And he would then be known as a *jindai,* or "War Substitute."

Concerning this there is an ancient practice. In such a case, though he takes the position of elder brother, he should think of the child as his own son, though actually his nephew, and should care for him and educate him accordingly. And in taking the place of the head of the house he should collect all the arms, armor, horse trappings, and various other possessions that belong to it and, with one or two other members of the family, should go over everything carefully and enter them all in a book.

扨其子恙なく成長致し。既に十五歳に罷成候においては。來年は
十六歳にも罷成候得ば。若輩ながらも。一騎前の御用には相立
可申候間。唯今まで手前へ被下置候知行を讓渡し。御奉公相勤
めさせ申度旨。書付を以て。急度願ひを相立候義尤に候。其節品
に依ては。願の通り尤には思召候得共。いまだ若年の義にも有之
間。先づ二三年の間は。其方相勤め候様になど。被仰付有まじき
に非ず。たとひ如何様の重き仰あり共。達て御理り申上。倅願の通
りと有之時は。其初調べ置たる帳面を以て。先代の諸道具不殘引
渡し。其身陣代を勤め罷在内に。調義致したる諸色の内にも。讓り
與へて可然品あらば。是をも帳面に記して相渡し尤に候。

且又右の通り家督被仰付刻。たとへば五百石本高の内。三百石
を甥に賜り。殘る二百石をば。數年陣代仕りたれば。其方へ被下
置など被仰出義も可有之。左様の節は。難有仕合身に餘り奉存候
得共。本家の知行高減じ候段。迷惑に存候間。何分にも兄が舊知
相違なく甥に仰付られ。私義は御暇被下置候様にと。達て願立可
申候。右のごとく候てこそ。陣代勤めたる武士の本意たるべきに。

もはや初陣を勤る程の年來に成たる甥に。家督を渡さず。或は家
督を渡し候ても。我が陣代を勤る内に。讓りの諸道具悉く紛失致
し。家居さへ住荒したるまゝ。修復も致さず。剩へ兄が讓らざる借
金買掛を仕て是を引渡し。猶其上に扶持米。合力金などのねだ
り言を申て。若輩なる甥の臑をかぢる分別を仕るは。不埒の至りと
可申候。初心の武士心得のため仍如件。

Then when the child has grown up to the age of fifteen, so that the next year he will become an independent cavalier among the younger retainers, it is proper that he petition his lord to be allowed to enter his service and have the salary that he had been granted paid to him. According to the quality of the child this petition may be granted, or it is possible that on account of his youth the guardian may be requested to serve a few more years. But, however urgent this suggestion may be, he should definitely refuse it, and when the petition is granted he should produce the inventory of the property that he made previously and hand over all the effects of the late father. He should add to the list and turn over any goods that he may have acquired while exercising his guardianship that it seems proper to relinquish.

Also, when he took over as head of the house the War Substitute may have had assigned to him part of the income, for instance two hundred *koku* out of a total of five hundred, the remaining three hundred being left for the nephew. This may have been a piece of luck for him but it is actually the reverse for the main house, whose estates and advantages were thereby diminished, so he must request that his elder brother's original income be assigned in full to the heir. Such is the proper conduct for a samurai who becomes a War Substitute.

By contrast, there is the one who is unwilling to hand over property to the heir when he comes of age, or when he does he leaves the property in bad condition and the house in disrepair and makes no attempt to restore them. Worse still, he may bequeath to the heir debts that his father had not contracted, in addition to pestering the young man continually for food and allowances and the like. Such a man is a rascal with no principles.

臨終

武士たらむものは。大小上下に限らず。第一の心掛たしなみと申す
は。其身の果際の善悪に止り申候。常々何程口をき〻。利根才覺に
見え候者も。今を限りの時に臨み。前後不覺に取亂し。最期悪しく
候ては。前方の善行は皆々水に成り。心ある人の下墨に預り。大き
に耻かしき事にて候。

武士の戰場に臨みて。武邊手柄の働を仕り。高名を極るも。兼て
討死と覺悟を極め置たる上の事にて候。去るに依て。時の運悪しく
勝負に仕負。敵に首を取らる〻時。我が名を敵に問れては。慥かに
姓名を名乘り。莞爾と笑て首をわたし。毛頭もわるびれたる氣色な
く。或は外科の療治に叶はぬ程の深手を負ても。正氣さへあれば。
番頭組頭。諸傍輩の聞前にて。慥に物をも申し。手負ぶりをたしな
み。尋常に相果候は。武士の正義第一の所に候。

The Latter End

The samurai, whether great or small, high or low, must rank before all other things the consideration of how to meet his inevitable end. However smart or capable he may have been, if he is upset and quaking in his boots and so behaves badly when he comes face to face with death, his previous good deeds will be like water in the sand and all decent people will despise him so that he will be covered with shame even as he dies.

For when a samurai goes out to battle and does valiant and splendid exploits and makes a great name, it is only because he made up his mind to die. And if unfortunately he gets the worst of it and he and his head must part company, when his opponent asks for his name he must declare it at once loudly and clearly and yield up his head with a smile on his lips and without the slightest sign of fear. Or if he is so badly wounded that no surgeon can do anything to save him, if he is still conscious, the correct procedure for a samurai is to answer the questions of his superior officers and comrades and inform them of the manner of his being wounded and then to make an end with no more fuss.

爰を以て考へ候得ば。靜謐の時代たり共。武士をたしなむものは。其身老人ならば申すに及ばず。たとひ年若く候ても。大病を受候に於ては覺悟を極め。今生に心懸りなる事の無之樣に致し。重き職役をも相勤るに於ては勿論の儀。たとひ輕き奉公の身たりといふとも。物のいはるゝ内。支配頭を招請致し。年來上の御厚恩に預り候得ば。いかさま一度は御用に相立申度と。常々心掛罷在候處。如此の重病に懸り。最はや本復難仕次第に罷成。近頃殘念に存候得共。今更是非に不及候。愈相果候に於ては。只今迄の御厚恩あり難き仕合に奉存旨。御家老中迄被仰上被下候樣にと申述尤に候。其義を濟したる上にて。一家朋友などへも。最後の暇乞を致し候刻。子供をも呼出し。我等義多年上の御厚恩を蒙りながら。病死を致すは。武士の本意に非ずといへ共。其段は是非に及ばざる所なり。

其方共義は年若ければ。我等が志を受繼。若自然の義も有之に於ては。是非上の御用に可相立と覺悟致し。常に忠義の志を勵まし。御奉公に精出し勤むべく候。もし此遺言に違ひ。不忠不義の仕形有之に於ては。草葉の陰に於ても。勘當と心得べしなど。急度遺言を仕り候は。眞の武士の正義に候。

聖人の詞にも。人の將に死なむとする。其云ふこと善と哉らん有之げに候。右のごとくにてこそ。武士の最期共可被申候。然るに迚も本復のならぬ病氣といふ思慮もなく。死がらかひを致し。病躰を人が輕くさへいへば悦び。重くいふをいやがり。あれのこれのと醫者悶着を仕り。叶はぬ祈念願立など申して。狼狽分別と成り。

In the same way, in times of peace the unswerving samurai, particularly if he is old but even if he is young and stricken with some serious disease, ought to show firmness and resolution and attach no importance to leaving this life. Naturally if he is in high office, but even if he occupies a low position, while he can still speak he should request the presence of his official superior and inform him that because he has long enjoyed his favor, he has consequently wished fervently to do everything in his power to carry out his duties, but unfortunately he has now been attacked by this serious disease from which it is hard to recover, and consequently is unable to do so; and that since he is about to die he wishes to express his gratitude for past kindness and trusts to be remembered respectfully to the clan's councilors. This done, he should bid farewell to his family and friends and explain to them that it is not right that a samurai should die of illness after having received great favors from his lord for so many years, but sadly in his case he can do nothing about it.

They who are young must carry on his loyal intentions and swear to do their duty to their lord, always increasing this loyalty so as to serve with all the strength they possess. If they fail to do this or act in any disloyal or undutiful way, then even from the shadow of the grass his spirit will disown and disinherit them. Such is the leavetaking of a true samurai.

And in the words of the Sage too it is written that when a man is about to die his words should be those that seem correct. This is what the end of a samurai should be, and how different is it from that of one who refuses to think of his illness as incurable and is worried about dying, who rejoices if people tell him he looks better and dislikes it if they say he looks worse, all the while he fusses with doctors and gets a lot of useless prayers and services said for him and is in a complete state of agitation and confusion.

病氣は次第に重るといへ共。何を一言申置事をも致さず。悉皆犬
猫の死も同然の有様にて。一生一度の臨終の致し損じを仕るは。
此書の始に申し斷り候。死を常に心に當ることを仕らず。人の死を
聞ては忌々敷と存じ。おのれはいつまでも此世に在る筈の様に覺
え。欲深く。生を貪る心より起る死ぞこなひに候。斯のごとき卑怯
の意地にて。戦場に臨み。忠義の一圖を以て。晴なる討死などの。
罷成べき義にては無之候。爰を以て武士をたしなむものは。疊の
上に於て病死を遂るを。一生一度の大事とは申すにて候。初心の
武士心得のため仍如件。

奉公

奉公を勤る武士。我が頼み奉る主君。何ぞ大きなる御物入さし集
ひて。御勝手向ひしと廻りかね。何共可被成様無之に至りて。常
々家中へ下し置る。知行切符の内を。いか程づ。何が年が間。御
借用に被成度など。有之義もなくては不叶候。其多少によらず。畏
りて御請を申上るより初ては。他人の義は申すに及ばず。たとひ女
房子供の寄合雑談の中に於ても。是は難義の至り。迷惑の仕合な
ど。言葉の端にも申出すは。武士の本意に非ず候。子細を申すに。
昔が今に至る迄。主君の御難義をば。家來共が打寄て是を見屆
奉り。家來の難義をば。主君の御力を以て救ひ被下候は。是皆定
れる武家の作法に候。頼み奉る主君の御内證御さし詰り。御手づ
かへと申すに至りては。公界へ懸り。是は大名役にて。不被成して
は叶はざる義までをも。大形はさし止められ。萬事を御堪忍被成
候を見奉るに付ては。御家來の身にて。氣の毒にも。口惜しくも。存
間敷様とては無之候。

As he gradually gets worse he says nothing to anyone but ends by bungling the one death he has so that it is no better than that of a dog or cat. This is because he does not keep death always before his eyes, as I recommended that he do in my first chapter, but brushes away any mention of it as a sign of bad luck and seems to think he will live forever, greedily hanging on to his existence. One who ventures into battle in this cowardly spirit is not likely to die a glorious death in a halo of loyalty, so that anyone who aspires to the samurai ideal should see that he knows how to die properly of illness on the mats.

Service

When a samurai is in service it may come to pass that his lord has to meet large expenses and his circumstances therefore become narrowed, so that he must borrow part of the salaries of his retainers for several years. In this case, whether the amount is great or small, it is highly improper for a samurai to suggest, or even hint in the privacy of his family, much less outside it, that this causes him any difficulty or embarrassment. Since the days of old it has been the custom for retainers to rally to their lord in his time of need, just as he has always been ready to help them in theirs. And when a lord is pressed by private liabilities so that it affects his public duties and prevents him from undertaking things that it is considered the business of a daimyo to do, and has to put up with a lot of annoyance as a result, this surely is a painful thing for his retainers to contemplate.

但常式の義は成次第とも可申候。只明日にも天下の國端に於て。不慮の騒動有之刻。相定れる軍役を以て。近日彼地へ發向あれ候樣にとの上意下り。すはや其支度とあるに及でも。先入用のものは金銀に候。然れば其才覺と有ても。何方よりも出所無之。石にて手を詰たると申す喩のごとくにて。跡へも先へも行兼る難義の内に。同列の大名衆は。用意相調ひ。來る幾日には必ず出馬と申合せ定り候ては。もはや延も縮もならざるに付。不足たらだらながらも。出勢なくては不叶候。

静謐の時代には。我も人も能見物と心得。市屋町屋を借りふさげ。野にも山にも立わたり。貴賤目晒しの武者押は。形のごとくの晴事なるに。家中の人馬出立共に。諸手に劣りて見苦しき様子ならば。主君大將の御身に取て。御一生の御恥辱是に過ず。此一大事を以て考へ候時は。家中大小の諸士。新參古參に限らず。拜領し罷在知行切符の内。分々相應に差上ずしては叶はず候。

然れば物成減少の年限の内は。隨分簡略仕り。人馬をも耗し。冬は紙子木綿の衣類。夏は布かたびらを着し。朝夕は黒米飯。糠味噌汁と分別を極め。自身は水を汲薪をさき。妻子に飯を爨せ力に稱ふ程は難義苦勞を致し。何卒主君の御用途を整へさせまゐらせ度と。一筋に存じ入候は。奉公の本意たるべく候。

Ordinary affairs can go on somehow, but suppose that tomorrow some unexpected disturbance happens on the frontier of the province and our contingent is ordered to start at once to take up some position. The first thing that would be needed is money. But however clever one may be, this commodity cannot be produced immediately. As the proverb has it, like a man with his hand caught under a stone who cannot move in any direction, it would be difficult to do anything in such a case. Yet the other daimyos will all be ready to start on the day appointed, which cannot be altered, so that even though we may be unprepared there is no escaping our setting out too.

In times of peace a military procession makes a brave show and people from the countryside come crowding into town to see it, so that it is exposed to the view of all classes. If our array of weapons and armor is inferior to the others, it will bring lifelong shame to the lord and his captains. So when we consider all this and its importance, all samurai—both great and small, old retainers and recently joined ones—must not fail to contribute a suitable proportion of their salary.

And during this period of reduced income everyone must use his brains a little and find ways to reduce the number of men and horses and to wear garments of cotton and paper in winter and unlined cotton *katabira* in summer. Then for the morning and evening meals only unpolished rice and rice bran and *misoshiru* soup must be eaten. And everyone must split his own wood and draw his own water and make his wife cook the rice and, in fact, endure every possible hardship without complaint. For those who are in the service of a lord have a duty to bend all their energies to keep his affairs in order.

且又右の通り艱難を仕り罷在年限の内たり共。何ぞ臨時の御用
を承り。非常の物入ある事も有べく候。左様の砌りは。自身の指
替。女房の手箱を質物に入ても。其償ひを致し。金銀拝借などを。
此方よりは願ふべからず候。子細を申すに。たとひ主君の御耳にこ
そ入らず共。家老年寄中の下墨にも。物成減少にあひたるを下心
に含み。武士に似合ざるねだり言を申と思はれては。重ねて口もき
かれずとのたしなみに候。初心の武士心得のため仍如件。

臣職

主君より恩祿を受。一騎役を勤る士は。此身をも命をも。我が物と
心得候ては事濟不申候。子細を申すに。武家の奉公人の内に。二
段の様子有之候。身輕き小人中間なんど申類の義は。晝夜共に身
の暇なく。手足に骨をば折候へ共。大切の一命は。必主君の御用
に立ねばならぬと申す定めは無之に付。合戰迫合の場所に於て。
未練の振舞有之候ても。強ち不屈との詮議も懸り不申候。然れば
身ばかりを賣切の奉公人共可申かにて候。

武士の義はそれとは違ひ。一命を奉る奉公人に候。抑主君はもと
變の御役人なれば。萬一世の變有之刻は。御身上相應の軍役有
之。譬ば十萬石の高にて。馬上百七十騎。弓足輕六十人。鐵炮足
輕三百五十人。鑓百五十本。旗二十本。これは公義より定め置る
ゝ所の軍役に候。

If we put up with these difficulties even in a period of economy, we can meet any special need of our lord and even raise some money for an emergency. One can, for instance, pawn his spare sword and even his wife's workbox, and with the value of these he will have enough without borrowing. Even if your lord does not get word of it, or the councilors and superior officers despise you for it, it is an unspeakable thing for a samurai to complain about the reduction of his salary.

A Vassal's Duty

A samurai who is a cavalier and has been granted a salary by his lord must not call his life or even his soul his own. Among those who render military service there are two types. First are the petty retainers and *chugen,* or attendants, and so on who have no leisure time either day or night but must work hard at all hours, but who are not necessarily bound to lay down their lives for their master and so cannot be blamed if they are not specially trained or skilled in martial exercises. For they are actually only employees who sell their labor as workers, and nothing else.

But the bushi or samurai is completely different, for he is a servant who gives his life, as well. His lord too is a similar vassal, though on a different scale. For should any trouble arise in the empire he must render military service suitable to his status. That is to say, if he has a feudal estate of 100,000 *koku* he has to provide 170 horsemen, 60 foot archers, 350 matchlock-men, 150 spearmen, and 20 banners, according to the statute of the shogun's government.

外に召連玉ふ人數は。其大將の御器量次第。又思召次第に候。
扨右の通相定れる軍役の人數を引つれ。御出陣あられたる跡とて
も。居城を持かためて。人に取られぬ樣に。相守る程の人數をば。
殘し置れずしては叶はず候。去るに依て。常々はさして御入用も無
之樣に候得共。大身小身へかけ。數多の士を抱へ置被成。家中多
き中には不器量沙汰の限り。或は五體不具なる生れ付。又は心行
不足に見ゆる者をも。大目に御覽被成て。父祖の知行を相違なく
下し置るゝ事に候。

然れば御家來の身にて勘辨致すべきは。日本國中國主城主多き
中に。いかなる宿縁ありてか主從の約をなし。似合相應の祿を賜
り。譬ば百石と申す少知にても。十年には千石の米高に罷成候
を。先祖の代より其身の代まで幾十年ともなく。拜領致し來りたる
俵子も積り候はゞ。凡如何程に可相成や。

The number of his men beyond this depends on his inclination and as well as the capacity of his commander. Beside this force that he will lead out to war he must also leave enough men behind in his castle town to protect it against attack. So that though he does not need them all the time he must maintain a large number of samurai of all kinds. And among these may be some who are poor fighters or who were born crippled or who seem wanting in spirit, but whose defects he generously overlooks so that they can continue to draw their hereditary salaries.

Therefore, what a retainer ought to bear in mind is how many retainers are kept by all the lords of provinces and castles in the whole Empire of Japan who are thus bound to their masters by such mutual ties of affinity and who are receiving from them considerable sums and perquisites, in that for instance such a small salary as a hundred *koku* will in ten years amount to a thousand *koku*. And if it has been paid for several generations to the family for many tens of years, what a very large sum will it not amount to?

此君恩の深きに報謝し奉らんには。常々の番役供役使役などは。治世の只居り役と申物にて。世並人並の義なれば。押立たる奉公とは申難し。只明日にもすはといふ時。平場の迫合ならば壹番鎗。敵城を攻るに於ては一番乗。もし味方利を失ひ引退く刻は殿。或は品に寄り敵の射る矢おもてに立塞りて。主君大将の御身代りにも罷立。或は其場を一足も引退かずして。晴なる討死をも遂なん。此義に於ては摩利支尊天も照覽あれ。人にさせては見まじき物をと。口廣くこそいはね。我が心ひとつに覺悟を極め罷在を。武士の奉公の奥意とは申候。扨右のごとく奥意を極むるうへは。我が身も命も我が物に非ずいつ何時主君の御用有べきも難計からは。彌身命を大切にかけ。大食大酒淫欲等の不養生を愼しみ。疊の上の病死をさへも本意と思はず。

ましてや喧嘩口論など仕出して友傍輩を打果し。我が身命を失ふ類ひの不忠不義は。深く愼しむしべき事に候。其愼の致方は。むざと口をきかぬがよく候。口をきくから起りて口論あり。口論がつのりては必ず雜言あり。武士と武士との出會にて。互ひの雜言に及びて後。無事なる事は。千萬に一つも無之候。去るに依て。最初口論に及ぶ時。其心得を致し。兼て主君へ捧げ置たる身命といふ義を存じ出し。抑へ控へを仕るを忠義の武士共申し。又は分別者共申にて候。初心の武士心得のため仍如件。

In return for all this great favor, the retainer does his ordinary peace-time duty as guard or company officer or inspector, a mediocre sort of performance that can hardly be called outstanding service. But at any time he may hear a sudden call to arms and then he may take his place in the ranks as a leading spearman, or, if it is an attack on a castle, as a vanguard horseman, or, if his side is driven back, as a rear guard in the retreat, or, if he is up to it, he may even take the place of his lord or commander and give his life for them under the arrowhail of the foe and die a noble death where he stands without yielding an inch. Then indeed does the samurai realize the deepest sense of service when he steels his resolution and shouts, "*Marishiten* be my witness, I will show you a deed that no other shall do!" And since to achieve this height of devotion he cannot call his body or soul his own, and he never knows when he may have to render such service to his lord, he must take care not to damage his health by overeating or drinking too much or sexual indulgence; neither must he regard death on the mats at home as his proper end.

Much more must he be on his guard against disputes and squabbles with his comrades that may lead to blows, and risk the useless waste of lives in a disloyal and undutiful manner. To this end it is essential to think carefully before you speak, for it is out of words that quarrels arise. And when quarrels grow hot, physical altercations are apt to follow, and when one samurai fights with another the affair can hardly end in a friendly manner. So if there is any risk of a dispute, remember that your life does not belong to you but to your lord, and control your temper so that the matter goes no further. Such is the duty of a discreet and loyal samurai.

武役

總じて武士の役義と申すは。陣普請兩役に候。天下戦國の時は。明ても暮ても爰の陣彼所の軍とて。一日たりとも武士としては。身を安く置事は不罷成候。陣とさへ申せば。普請は附合にて。爰の要害。彼所の堀切扱は取手陣城付城など申て。晝夜にかぎらぬ急ぎの普請に。上下の骨折辛勞は淺からざる義に候。

治世に於ては。陣といふ事なければ。それに從て普請とても無之候。去るに依て。武將の下。大小の士に。番役供役使役等。其外役々を定められ。諸人只居役の勤をさせて指置被成候を。是が武士の役義ぞと心得。肝要の役義たる。陣普請の兩役の義をば曉の夢にも思ひ出さず。たまさかにも公義御普請の御手傳。主君へ仰付られ。其物入多きを以て。家中の士へ割合になり。少しづゝ出金有之時は。何ぞ出すまじき物を出すがごとく。悔みつぶやき候は。畢竟武士の役義に於ての肝要は。陣普請といふを。存じ辨へざるより起る事に候。

The Duties of Samurai

Samurai fulfill duties that are twofold: military and constructive. When the land is at war, he must be in the camp and the field both day and night and can never know a moment's rest. Construction is associated with the camp, for what with its strongholds and moats and embattled camps and fortified outposts all ranks have to work all the time as fast and as furiously as possible.

But in peaceful times there is no camp duty and consequently none of the construction connected with it. Then the various ranks of samurai under their commanders are appointed to fixed duties as guards, escorts, inspectors, and the like. They come to regard these stay-at-home functions as the normal ones for a warrior family, and think of field service as nothing but a distant dream. Then, whenever the honor of assisting the shogun's government in its buildings is conferred on the daimyos, and the expense of this is so great that they must pass some of it onto their retainers and they therefore request a contribution of a percentage of their salaries, the samurai begrudge it and grumble about it as though it were an tax or fee. They do not realize that to take part in both military and constructive activities is the regular business of samurai.

扨常式の番役供役使役の義も。我が當り前の本番を勤るをさへ。大きなる難義と心得。させる病氣と申にても無之にも。病氣斷りを申立て。同役相番へ助を賴み。人に苦勞を懸るをば何共存ぜず。或は旅がけの使には。路銀の物入。道中の骨折を厭ひて作病を起し。其物入苦勞を人に讓り。諸傍輩の下墨を憚る事もなく。其外間近き所の使といへ共。日の中に二度とも出るか。又は風雨劇しき時などは。友傍輩の聞前にて遠慮もなく。役にも立たぬよまひ言などを申。骨を折ながら意地むさき勤方を仕るは。悉皆士の皮をかぶりたる。小者中間に均しき樣子に候。

戰國に生れ合たる武士は。毎度軍に罷立。夏の炎天には具足の上よりほし付られ。冬の寒風には。具足肌を吹透され。雨に打れ雪をかぶりて。野にも山にも鎧の袖を敷寢に仕り。剩へ飲食ふ物とても。黑米飯鹽汁より外には無之仕合にて。或は對陣城攻。又は籠城等の辛苦を仕るは。難義共苦勞共。只尋常の事にては有べからず候。

爰を以て考へ候時は。靜謐の時代に生れ合。夏は蚊帳をたれ。冬は夜着蒲團にまかれ。朝夕好み喰をいたして。安樂に渡世仕るは。大きなる仕合に候。然れば座敷の内の番役。近所の供役使役などの。苦勞太義に思はれべき道理とては無之候。甲州武田家の老臣。弓矢功者と呼れし。馬場美濃と申たる士は。戰場常在と申す四字を書て壁間に懸置。平生の受用と仕候由申傳ひ候。初心の武士心得のため仍如件。

So you find some regarding their ordinary peacetime duties as an extreme hardship and putting in a medical excuse even when nothing is the matter with them, and heedless of the trouble they cause others who are asked to take their place. Then again, if they are sent out as a traveling inspector they resent the journey's fatigue and the expense incurred, so they submit a note from the doctor for that also, and hand off the trouble and expense onto their comrades without being in the least bit ashamed of the contempt they earn. And even if the place where they are sent is nearby, they complain openly about having to go out to it twice in one day, or else about the poor state of the weather. People who do their duty in this mean spirit, as though it were only a burden, are nothing but low-down grooms and servants in the skins of samurai.

The warriors born in the age of civil war were always in the field, scorched in their armor under summer skies or pierced through its chinks by winter blasts, soaked by the rain and cloaked by the snow, sleeping on boggy land or on a hill with no pillow but their chainmail sleeve and with nothing to eat or drink but unhulled rice and salt soup. Whether they had to fight in the field or to attack or defend a fortress they thought it no special hardship or trial, just all in a day's work.

When we reflect on this and how we, born in times of peace, can sleep under a mosquito net in summer and wrap ourselves in quilts in winter, and indeed live at ease eating whatever we like at any time of day, we should consider ourselves lucky indeed. But there is no reason why we should regard indoor guard duty or going out to check on the neighborhood as a serious burden. There was a certain Baba Mino, a veteran of renown under the house of Takeda of Kai, who wrote out and hung up on the wall as his life's maxim the four characters that signify "The field of battle is my normal abode."

謹愼

主君の御定紋の付たる御小袖。又は上下など拝領致し候ものは。御紋付の小袖を着用の時は。自分の紋付の上下を着し。御紋付の上下も着し候はゞ。小袖は定めて自分の紋付を着し候心得尤に候。然るに小袖も上下も一様に。御紋付を着し候ては。主君の御親類方に均しき様子なれば。主君へ對し奉り慮外に候。右拝領の小袖上下。古く成て着用ならぬ時は。御紋所は切抜て燒捨可申候。御紋を汚すまじとの愼しみに候。

扨又近所に罷在傍輩の中に。重き病人。又は憂事など有之においては。たとひ其者と心易からぬ挨拶たり共。高笑音曲等堅く相愼しみ。妻子召使などへも其段急度可申付事に候。其者のおもはくばかりにも無之。不遠慮もの不作法者と。諸傍輩の下墨を慮ての愼しみに候。初心の武士心得のため仍如件。

Circumspection

Anyone who receives from his lord a present of a *kosode* or *kamishimo* with the lord's crest on it should be careful, when he wears the small-sleeved robe, to put on a *kamishimo* with his own crest over it, or if it is the *kamishimo* with his lord's crest that he wears then he should don a *kosode* with his own crest. For if he wears a garment with the lord's crest only, it might look as though he were a relative, and that would be impolite. And when these garments with the lord's crest become too old to be worn any longer, the crests should be cut off them and burned, so that they may not become soiled and treated disrespectfully.

And when any of your neighbors is either very ill or suffering from some bereavement, even though you may not be intimate friends, take care not to indulge in any music or loud laughter, and give orders to your family and servants to do the same. This is not only because of what they may think but also to avoid the shame of being despised by neighbors and comrades as a boor with no manners.

言辭

奉公仕る武士。主君より大切の仕もの。放討など仰付らるゝ時は。
御家中人多き中に。今度の御用を私へ仰付らるゝ段。武士の冥理
に相叶ひ。忝次第に存ずる旨。成程潔よく御請を申上る心得尤に
候。然るを生温き御請に及ぶは。以の外宜しからず候。

Using Words

It is most appropriate for a samurai in active service, on receiving an order to carry out an especially important task, such as an "execution at large" (*hanashiuchi*), to bravely accept forthwith saying, "For me, one of many candidates in the lord's employ, to be given this task is to fulfill my destiny as a warrior, a most welcomed honor, which I accept with gratitude." However, it is totally out of the question to respond to the request in a timid and halfhearted way.

子細を申すに。内心には勇氣を勵し。天晴仕すまして御目に懸べきと存じ詰候ても。勝負は時の運によれば討損じ。剰へ返り討に逢事も有之候。何れも後日に至り。諸傍輩の中において。善惡の批判有べき事に候。其首尾好ければ。いかさま御請の砌より。仕り兼まじき氣色に見えたるが。能は仕濟したりと申して。諸人譽事に仕候。

もし又仕損じて返り討に逢候時も。右の御請の次第を申出て。中々仕り損ずる樣なる者にては無かりしが。如何致して討損じけるぞと申して。各悔みて惜み申候。

扨又少しにても鈍き御請を仕り候時は。たとひ好首尾に致し濟し候ても。偏に時の運のよき也と申して。誰も左のみ譽不申候。

もしも致し損じたる時は。右御請の砌から。何とやらん覺束なく思はれしが。果して仕損ひたりと申して。諸人謗るものにて候。

爰を以て何分にも御請をば。潔よくとは申にて候。總じて武士をたしなむ者は。假初にも。仕形の負を取らぬ樣にとの心懸第一に候。

Specifically, even though you know that you have worked up the requisite courage, and fully intend to do a splendid job and then have an audience with your lord, wining and losing depend on chance. There is always the possibility that you will fail in the attack, or that your opponent will succeed in an attack on you instead. Either way, there will come a day when, among your comrades, judgments of right and wrong will be made. If the whole thing is well-received, of course, both the acceptance and the execution of the job will be viewed in a positive light, and people will praise you, saying, "He accomplished his task well."

But if you fail in its execution and, worse, a successful counterattack occurs, people will say that judging by the way you accepted the assignment you didn't seem to be someone who was likely to fail. And they will express their condolences and regrets.

However, if there was any sign of timidity or indirection when you accepted the assignment, the whole job may indeed conclude without a hitch, but success will be partly attributed to chance and no one will give full credit to you.

And in the event of a failure, you will be maligned by others as a man who from the time you accepted this assignment appeared to be ineffective, so there will be little wonder it ended badly.

Therefore, you should bravely and directly agree to undertake whatever assignment you are given. In short, someone who is fully dedicated to being a warrior understands that steering clear of even the slightest bit of failure in his work is his first priority.

譬ば人に無心合力などを云懸られ候ても。是は成る事成らぬ事と
をば。幾重にも分別致し成まじきと思ふ事ならば。それは格別。既
に得心致す程ならば。如何にも潔よく請合候てこそ。先の者も別て
過分共可存候を。請口鈍く。不肖不肖の様子に見ゆる時は。向の
者の心に成ては。過分氣も薄く。何とぞ可成ならば。此仁へばかり
は。無心を云ぬ様に致し度事かなと。無念にも。口惜くも。不存して
は不叶候。如此なるを。意地のきたなき共申し。切離れのなき共申
し。損の上の損共申候。

初心の武士心得のため仍如件。

譜牒

奉公を勤る武士。古參の義は申すに及ばず。たとひ昨今の新參者
たり共。主君の御家の起り。御先祖御代々の義。或は御親類御縁
者方の御つゞきは申に及ばず。家中においても。世間の人にも知ら
れたる。名高き傍輩の噂などをば。古老の者に問尋て。覺悟致し
罷在義尤に候。子細を申に。他家の者に參會談話の刻。我が主人
の家の義を尋に逢ひ。それも存ぜず。是をも不承と申ては。大躰よ
き奉公人と見ゆる者も。是が爲に手淺く思ひなさるゝものにて候。
初心の武士心得のため仍如件。

For example, if he is asked by others for assistance, he will make several attempts to determine whether the work is something that he can bring to a conclusion or not. Furthermore, if he thinks it is something he should not do on moral grounds, then he rejects it directly. In agreeing to do a favor, no matter what it is, if your acceptance is brave and immediate, then the person who made the request will be all the more grateful. But when your reply is timid and indirect, seeing you hesitate, the one who asks your help feels little in the way of gratitude and will make every effort to avoid asking you to help him again. It is a regrettable and disappointing situation, but one that you should understand. Call it hedging, call it lack of decisiveness, or call it failure upon failure.

These words are for the edification of those who have resolved to become true samurai.

Records

A samurai in service, whether one who has lately joined a household, or a veteran retainer, should be sure to make himself well versed in the history of his lord's family, its origin, its ancestral records and its connections, as well as in the accounts of the deeds of any of his comrades who have distinguished reputations. This he should do by inquiring about them from the senior members of the clan. For if he does not do so, when he meets outsiders and in the course of talking turns out to be ignorant of these matters, even if he is thought to be a good retainer in all other respects, he will be held in little esteem.

陪従

奉公を勤る武士。主君御旅行の御供を致し。泊りへ着候に於て
は。其所の者をかたらひ。近所に見ゆる。山林寺宮などを目當にし
て。東西を問尋ね。御本陣より何方に當りて。いか様の廣き場所有
之。道筋はケ様とまでをも。日の暮前に何となく見分致し。篤と心
得罷在義肝要に候。子細は。夜中急火などの節。主君俄に御立退
被成刻。御先に立て。御案内可申上が為に候。

扨又其身歩行にて御供を勤る節は。上り坂にては御先に立。下り
坂にては御跡に立心得などは。尤軽き事ながらも奉公の一つに
候。右の如くの義を以て。手懸りと致し思案をめぐらし。迚も奉公
を勤る身と罷成からは。何がな一奉公もがなと。朝暮油断なく心
掛勵み候は。武士の本意に候。初心の武士心得のため仍如件。

Escort

When a samurai in service accompanies his lord on a journey and they arrive at an inn where they will spend the night, it is most important that he should before sunset take care to talk with the people of the locality, and note any hill or wood or shrine or temple and take his bearings by them, and find out in which direction from their lodging there is an open space and what is the condition of the road. This should be done so that, if a fire suddenly breaks out during the night and his lord must escape the inn, he will be able to lead the way and know where to guide him.

When he accompanies his lord on foot, he will remember to go in front of him up a hill and behind him down a slope. This may seem a small matter, but it is one that a retainer should not overlook. For it is the duty of a samurai to be vigilant and alert at all times to think about and anticipate how he can render any possible service in the calling to which he was appointed.

有司

白無垢の小袖と役人とは。新らしき内がよきと申習はし候は。輕き
世話ながらも。一段尤の事と覺え候。子細は白小袖の新らしき内
は。隨分暉麗なる物にて候得共。久しく着用致す時は。襟廻り袖口
の邊よりよごれ初めて。程なく鼠色の如くなりては。見苦しく手むさ
き物にて候。倩亦事に懸り候役人の義も。新役人の内は。萬づうひ
うひ敷。主君の仰付の趣を。大切に守り詰て。假初の義をも大事と
存じ。就中其役儀に付ての誓詞罰文の趣を心に懸て。違背致さぬ
様にと恐れ愼しみ候故。諸事の勤め方殘る所無之候。

去るに依て。無欲正直なる好役人かなと。家中一同の譽事に逢候
者も。其役儀を久しく勤めて。萬づ合點するに隨ひ。うかべ功者に
成り。新役人の時無之不調法をも致し候。それのみならず。新役の
時は。人より贈る音物をば誓詞の旨に任せて手際よく返し。もし不
受して叶はざる子細あれば受納致して。後日に相當の返禮を致す
など。扨も潔よき仕方かなと申す内。いつの程よりか分別相違仕
り。今此役義勤る内。少しなり共握りためんといふ欲心起るといへ
共。今まで音物は受ぬとて。手際よく返したるうへには。今更受納
致しがたきといふ底意は。色にもあらはれ。言葉の端にも聞ゆるを
以て。人も賢くて底意を悟り。表向は搆はぬふりにて。或は内縁に
便り。又は種々の手段を以て。物を贈ればいか程も受納を遂げ。其
返禮には。上を掠めて。依怙贔屓の沙汰に及ぶ外無之候。

Officials

A saying has it that officials and white garments are both best when new. Though it is only a joke I think it is true. For a white *kosode* robe looks extremely beautiful when new, but after it has been worn for some time first the collar and sleeve edges get soiled and then it soon becomes a dirty rat-color and looks terribly unpleasant. So too officials, when they are fresh on the job and inexperienced, obey their lord's orders punctiliously and pay attention to the slightest detail, because they respect the oaths they took on themselves and fear to violate them and thus invoke penalties.

In this way they serve without greed or dishonesty and are spoken well of by all their clan. Yet after they have held office for a long time they are likely to count on people's tacit acceptance of their actions and get a high opinion of themselves, so that they do rude things they would never have done previously. And further, when they were new to office they would only touch and then send back presents that they were given, as their oath of service requires. Or, when there was some special reason why they must receive them, before long they would make a return gift of equal value. However, after a while, a greedy spirit begins to grow in them, and while still declaring that they will take nothing and while appearing to behave with honesty they some-how make known that this is only an act. They soon overcome their apparent scruples and accept such presents, and as a return favor cannot help robbing the government and handing down decisions that benefit certain people.

此よごれ様と申は。かの白小袖の鼠色になりたるを見るに均しき
様子に候。但し白小袖のよごれ候は。身の垢と。ごみほこりの汚に
候得ば好灰汁を以て洗ひさへ致し候へば。随分暉麗になり申候。
人の心には種々様々の物が染込其よごれ深く候に付。只大形に洗
ひすゝぎたる分にては。暉麗にはなり兼申候。其上白小袖の義は。
年に一度か二度洗ひ候ても事濟み申候。人の心の洗濯と申は。二
六時中行住坐臥。事々物々の上に於て。或はもみあらひ。又はふり
すゝぎ。油斷透間なく致し候ても。又其跡からよごれ易く。けがれ易
きものにて候。白小袖のすゝぎ洗濯には灰汁に品々習ひ有之候。
其ごとく武士の心の洗濯を仕るに付ても。灰汁に習ひ有之候。

習ひは何ぞなれば。忠義勇の三つに候。其垢の様子によりて。忠貞
の灰汁にて落す垢も有之。節義の灰汁にて落すも有之候。右の如
く忠を以てあらひ。義を以てすゝぐといへども。其よごれ強くして落
かね候時は。勇猛の灰汁を加へて。力を出し無二無三にもみ洗ひ
候て。さつぱりと濯ぎあげ候は。是武士の心のせんたくの至極の秘
事に候。初心の武士心得のため仍如件。

And this corruption is just like the dirty color of a white garment, but where they differ is that this dirt can be washed away with lye or strong soap, whereas the stain on a man's heart gets so ingrained that it can hardly be removed. And if a garment is washed two or three times a year, that is enough, but a man's heart must ever be cleansed and scoured and rinsed, sleeping and waking, every day of the year without letup, and even then it is easily soiled. And precisely as lye and good technique in using it are needed for garments, so are they also needed for cleansing the hearts of samurai.

The practice here is that of the three principles of Loyalty, Duty, and Valor, while the lye must vary to suit the nature of the dirt. Some soiled hearts will yield to the soap of fidelity and some to that of constancy. Yet, though you may apply loyalty or duty, certain dirt is so ingrained that it will not be washed out even then. But if to these principles be added valor and intense application to their use, then the corrupt behavior can be removed entirely. This is the most profound secret of the purification of the samurai heart.

假威竊威

奉公いたす武士の上には。主君の威を假ると申す義も有之。又主君の威を竊むと申す義も有之候。主君の御身の上にても。家來に威を貸し被成と申義も有之。又家來に威を竊まれさせ玉ふと申義も有之候。其故如何となれば。何ぞ重き職役に預る武士。其身年若きか。又は小身なるか。扨は家中の風俗。時の樣子に因りては。主君の威光を笠に着て。相働かねばならぬ事有之。本より上の御爲なるを以て。しばらく主君の威光を借受。其事を取計らひ候。是を名付て主君の威を假るとは申すにて候。主君の威光を借り奉り諸人の用ひも出來。御用の辨じ候程にさへ相成り候はゞ。早速其威光を返進仕り。自分其職役相當り權を以て。愼み勤めてこそ尤の義なるを。諸傍輩を初め。他所他門の者までも。誰殿の御内の誰さまと申す尊敬に預。内證の強みも有之を以て。欲心にひかれ。終には主君の威光をかり取に仕る。是を名付て主の威を盜むと申候。

Borrowed and Stolen Authority

A samurai in service may be said to have borrowed his master's authority and also to have robbed him of it. Similarly, his lord may lend it to him or let him steal it. When a retainer holds an important office, if he is young or of low rank he may be embarrassed by social customs or the current fashion and have to carry out his duties under color of his master's authority. He thus holds it temporarily for his lord's advantage. This is borrowed authority, and if he uses it to fulfill his lord's intentions and benefit the people and then returns it, he will have used it rightly in doing his duty prudently. But if, when he finds his comrades and even outsiders treating him with respect and addressing him as "Your Excellency" and "Your Honor" and so on, he becomes greedy for that dignity and reluctant to part with it, then he may be described as one who steals it.

扨又主君の御身も威光を家來に借して。威勢の付様に被成候は。古しへの明君賢將達の上にも。其例いか程も有之候。是を名付て家來に威を借すと申候。已に其御用も足り候節は。そろそろ御取返し不被成しては不叶候處に。御心永くいつまでも便々と貸置被成候から事起りて。後々は取返し惡き様に罷成り。つまりは借取に値被成候。是を名付て家來に威を盗まるゝと申候。是は主君の御身にとりて。大きなる御恥辱と申すばかりにも無之。數々の御損も有之事に候。家來に威勢が付過ぎ候へば。おのづから主君の御威光は薄くなり。何もかも家來次第の様に罷成。あの人さへ能呑込て合點なれば。御上の儀は事濟み埒も明くと心得。一家中の諸士。其者の機嫌を取事を肝要と仕り。主君の御事をば。假令の様に存ずるを以て。主從の親しみも離れ。自然と家中に忠義の武士の出來可申様も無之。萬一事の變到來の節。好人に事を欠なされ候。

扨外樣向の士は申すに及ばず。主君の側近く奉公致し。或はおとなしき役義を勤むる士までも。彼壹人の權威に抑れ。すくみかへりて罷在仕合なれば。是は御爲宜しからずと心付たる事とても。一言申出す事罷りならず。或は心底に悔み。扨は心安き友傍輩と。呟きつぶやき候へ共。誰有て進み出。主君の御聞に達し候者無之故。其者の我儘依怙晶屓。内證の榮耀の程。御存じあるべき様も無之。何もかも其者の致す義をば。宜しきとばかり思召。御油斷の上に於て。大きなる御難義にも及び。且は人をよく御存じなきは。主君大將の御人柄には似合不申と。世の謗りも必定に候。

Regarding the other aspect of a lord who lends his authority and gives his prestige to retainers, we find that in ancient times great nobles and famous commanders did this, to a certain extent. And when they should have required this authority to be given back when the task was finished, sometimes because of their easygoing nature they allowed it to be kept for some time, and then an incident arose that made it difficult to get it back without paying a price for it. Here their retainers certainly robbed them of their authority. This not only is a great disgrace to a lord but causes him great damage too. For if retainers gain too much power, that of their master is thereby decreased. And if people come to think they can get what they want by honoring the vassal because he controls all access to the lord, they will only think of getting into his good graces and will regard the lord as of secondary importance. In this way the benevolent relations of master and retainer will disappear and loyal samurai will become conspicuous by their absence. Then, if some emergency arises, there will be no good men left to deal with it.

Moreover, not only the outside retainers but also those in personal attendance on the lord, as well as those in some quiet offices, will feel oppressed by the authority of such a person, so that they will feel their heart squeezed, and this also is not good for their lord. For they will say nothing about things they ought to notice, but only regret it in their hearts and grumble privately to their friends without ever standing up and reporting it to their master. So the arbitrary conduct and partiality of the offender, as well as the extent of his honor and glory, remain unknown to his lord, who only thinks well of all he does and thus inadvertently brings great misfortune on his house. The incapacity to know what people truly are is generally condemned as not worthy of those who are lords or commanders.

其上彼者は。主君の御耳目をさへ恐れ憚らぬ心からは。ましてや
諸傍輩の氣をかね。おもはくを憚る義とては曾て無之。小役人共
を愛付け。たとへば我が知る人近付の許へ。付届けを致すにも。主
人の物入に致し遣はし。其向より返禮に來る音物をば。我が手前
へとり込。其外來客を饗應とても。主君の御臺所より。酒の肴の茶
の菓子のと申して持運ばせ。主の物は我が物。我が物は我が物と
申す如くの仕形なれば。畢竟は主君の御勝手の弱りともなり。是
亦御損の一つに候。右の次第を能々了簡致し主君の御念比ふか
く。御目をかけ被成に付ては。猶々我が身を謙り。心の驕りを抑へ
愼しみ。兎にも角にも主君の御威光の。耀く様に仕る義肝要に候。
忠臣は君有る事を知て。身有る事を知らず。とやらん申す古語も有
之由に候。初心の武士心得のため仍如件。

In addition, a man of this sort who cares nothing about what his lord thinks is unlikely to care about his comrades' opinion of him. He will favor the petty officials and give those who are his friends and acquaintances various fees and bribes not of his master's property while taking their return presents for himself. And when he entertains his guests he has the fish and liquor and cakes brought from his lord's kitchen. Thus acting on the belief that "what is my lord's is mine, and what is mine is my own," he weakens his master's estate and causes him great loss. Ponder all this very deeply therefore, and remember always to be humble and suppress all pretensions when your lord grants you any privilege at all, so that nothing may dim the brightness of his glory. As the ancient saying has it, "The loyal retainer does not realize his own existence, but only that of his lord."

聚歛

奉公仕る武士。御勝手向に懸りたる諸役の義は。いかにも難義な
るものに候。子細を申すに。其家中大小の奉公人を初め。城下の
町人。郷村の百姓に至るまで。迷惑不仕して。主君の御爲に罷成
やう取まかなひ候は。大方の智慧才覺にては難成事に候。一筋に
主君の御爲と存ずる時は。下の諸人の難義迷惑と成り。又下つ方
の悦ぶ様にばかり仕候ては。上の御勝手に悪く相成り。何れぞ一
方へ障り出來申ものに候。其上いか程利根才覺に生れ付たる武
士の心にも。貪欲と申す病氣は付安きものなる故。主君の御勝手
向を取まかなひ。諸人の用ひに預り。金銀のやりくりも自由になり
候へば。頓て奢り生じ。身のはゞも致し度相成るに付。工夫をめぐ
らし。主君の物をとり込。分に過たる家普請道具集め。振廻數寄な
どを仕る。是を名付けて盗臣と申候。

On Tax Extortion

The duties connected with his lord's treasury are the most trying for a samurai in service. With only common knowledge and ability, it is a great problem to know how to do well for one's master without causing some hardship to the other retainers, to say nothing of the farmers in the country and the citizens in the castle town. If you think solely of your lord's interests, the lower people will have much to put up with. Or, if you try only to make their lot comfortable, your master will not be so well off, and there is sure to be an imbalance somewhere. Further, however clever and shrewd a samurai may be by nature, the disease of covetousness or greed is easy to catch. If he must make arrangements to raise money for his lord's household and for other expenses and then has control of it, he may become self-important and extravagant and may even scheme to embezzle his lord's money, to build houses and collect curios and make an elegant appearance. This is the sort known as a thieving retainer.

扨又主君の御爲と申て。前代の仕置の筋に違ひたる新法の簡略
を仕出して。家中の難儀迷惑と罷成勘辨もなく。城下の町人には
過役をあて。郷村の百姓には高免を仕懸。或は向後仕置の邪魔に
成り。民の煩となるならぬ考へにも及ばず。當分眼前の利潤と見ゆ
る義のみを工夫仕出し。分別不足なる家老年寄出頭人などを。だ
まし勸めて是を呑込せ。其取成を以て。筋なき加增褒美を申受。も
しも其新法不益にして不調法になる時は。件の家老年寄の差圖
損ひの如く仕なして。己は其人の陰に隱れて罪科をのがれ。迷惑
致さぬ分別を仕る。如此なるを名付て聚斂の臣と申候。

右に申す盜臣の義は。武士に似合ざる主君の物を盜み取。不屆沙
汰を限りたる義とは申ながらも。天罰を蒙り。それが顯はれ候て。
身命を喪ぼし。其者壹人獨り轉びをさへ仕れば。事濟埒も明て。
諸人の難義迷惑となる事もなく。勿論仕置の邪魔。國土の煩にも
罷成義は。左のみ無之ものにて候。聚斂の臣と申す者は。普く人の
傷みになる義をあみ出し。重ねて致し直しの成兼る樣なる。國家政
道の邪魔になる義をも。致し初る物にて候へば。たとひ己が身につ
く私欲取込を致さず共。罪科此うへ有べからず候。

Again, there is the official who makes a new system different from that of the former lord, asserting that it is for his master's benefit, without caring what hardship it causes his colleagues. He makes the citizens of the castle town pay higher dues, and levies larger land taxes on the farmers, all the while thinking of getting more revenue in the immediate future with no regard for the people's comfort. Also he may deceive incompetent councilors and elders and chiefs of departments so that they agree to grant him improper increases in salary and rewards. But if these new regulations prove unworkable and ineffective, he will hint that they really were planned by these councilors and chiefs, and so avoid punishment by hiding behind their backs. This sort is known as the tax-extorting retainer.

Now as to the previously mentioned thieving retainers, though they make off with their lord's treasure in a way unworthy of a samurai and pervert justice accordingly, when heaven's punishment falls on them and they suffer personal ruin as they are themselves overthrown, the matter is ended, for the people are no longer oppressed and the trouble in the administration and loss to the province also ceases. But the tax-extorting official produces a much more extensive injury, which takes more effort to repair. Even if personal greed and embezzlement are not involved, damage to the administration of the country is the greatest possible crime.

さればこそ古賢の言葉にも。聚斂の臣あらむよりは。むしろ盗臣あ
れと有之げに候。抑武士の身にとりて。盗臣の名を蒙るより外に。
重き悪事は無之様に存じ候得共。右の詞を承り候へば。罪科の至
極は聚斂の臣に止り申候。然れば盗臣の科に首を斬り候に於て
は。聚斂の臣をば。磔にも懸申度物にて候。但古へは聚斂の臣と
盗臣とは。別々の様子なればこそ。聚斂の臣よりは。盗臣を勝しか
といふ批判も相聞え候。近世に至り候ては。聚斂の臣にして。而も
又盗臣の所行をも相兼。表向は。主人の御爲を致す面を致して。
内證は己が勝手になる様にばかり調義仕る。是を聚斂盗臣を合せ
たる大賊とは申にて候。箇様の大罪人の義ならば。いか様の罪科
に申行ひて可然か。批判に及びがたく候。初心の武士心得のため
仍如件。

頭支配

番頭支配頭の下に付て。奉公勤る小身の武士。我が頭たる面々の
心入。又は組あたりの善悪の義は。其身に引受。能合點致し罷在
るに付。我々など若も武士の冥理に叶ひ。立身を遂げて。組をも預
かる仕合にも罷威に於ては。組下の面々を。形の如く勞はり懐け
て。主君の御用に相立べし。勿論依怙贔屓などは。毛頭も仕るまじ
き物をと。人々存ずる物に候。然れ共其身段々立身致して。番頭支
配頭になり上り候へば。前方の心入とは相違致すものにて候。

Therefore do the sages of old declare that it is better to have a thieving official than a tax-extorting one. And though there can be nothing worse for a samurai than to gain a reputation as an embezzler, the ancients condemn the extortioner more. So if the thief is punished by beheading, the extortioner ought to be bound to a cross. This may have been the judgment of former times, but at the present day, because the actions of both may be regarded as the same—namely, feathering their nest while pretending to work for their lord's benefit—both are considered to be equally monstrous criminals. And for such a great offense it is not easy to find an adequate penalty.

On Becoming a Thief

Small retainers who serve under a guard captain or superintendent have to put up with being attentive to their various superiors and at the same time tolerant of their comrades' unequal abilities. But if they have the good fortune to be promoted and given charge of a company themselves, they should be sympathetic and considerate to those under them while also fulfilling their duty to their lord. It is perhaps unnecessary to say that they should not show favoritism or be shameless flatterers, but if in the course of time they rise to the positions of guard captain or superintendent, their former attitude is likely to change.

織田家の佐久間。羽柴家の魚住など申す輩。小身の時は。随分の
好武士に候ひしが。大身と成て後。分別相違致して。主君の見かぎ
りを蒙り。身上亡び候。是等よき先證と存候。初心の武士心得の
ため仍如件。

懈惰

主君を持たる武士。初條にも申述る如く。今日在て。明日を知らぬ
身命に候得ば。日毎にけふを奉公のいたし納めとさへ覺悟仕れ
ば。物に退屈もなく。諸事を投やりにも不仕。何事も皆其日拂ひに
仕るを以て。不念失念と申義も無之道理に候。然るに行末永き奉
公と存ずるから事起りて。物に退屈仕り。それより心もゆるみ氣も
怠り。事の緩やかなる義は申すに及ばず。たとひきはきはと相談を
遂て。埒を明ずしては叶はざる事も。それは明日の義。是は重ねて
の事と。打やり投やりに仕り。或は同役仲間にても。彼方へはね。
此方へぬり。誰ひとり身に引懸て。世話のやき手もなければ。諸事
はいやが上にかさなりつかへて。不埒なる事のみ多く成行候は。是
皆行末の月日を。頼みに存ずるより起る過ちにて。尤恐れ愼しむべ
き事に候。

For instance, Sakuma, vassal of Oda, and Uozumi, vassal of Hashiba, were examples of men who were admirable when humble samurai, but who deteriorated when they rose to high office and so were tossed aside by their lords and ruined.

Laziness

A samurai in service, as I said in the first chapter, must be one who lives for today but cares nothing for tomorrow. With that attitude, if he does what he must do day by day, with tireless devotion and thoroughness, so that nothing at all is left undone, he has no reason to feel any disgrace or regret. But troubles arise when people rely on the future and become lazy and indolent and let things slide, putting off urgent affairs after a lot of discussion—not to mention less-important ones—in the belief that they can just as well be done tomorrow. They push a job off onto one comrade and blame another for that, trying to get someone to do it for them. If there is no one to assist, they leave it undone so that before long a lot of unfinished jobs have accumulated. This is a mistake that comes from relying on the future, a practice of which one must be wary.

たとへば月幾日と。番日の定れる勤めならば。我が宿所よりの道法
と。日の長短とを考へ計り。交代の時刻より。少し早めに出候様に
心得べく候。迚も出べき勤番所へ。出がらかひを仕り。茶を一服。
煙草を一ぷくと申てぶらつき。或は女房子共と。一口づゝの雑談に
時を移して。宿を遅く出ては俄に狼狽。行違ふ人の見さかひもなき
程道を急ぎ。大汗を流して番所へ馳付。寒中にも扇を遣ひながら。
ちと不叶用事有りて。遅く罷出候などゝ。利口がましく申すなどは。
空氣たる事と可申候。

武士の勤番と申すは警衛の義なれば。何様の義たりといふ共。私
用を以て遅参に及ぶべき義は無之候。扨又右の心得を以て。我が
身はいつとても早く出勤致すといへ共。相手替りの傍輩の遅く出る
を待兼。もゝ尻に成りて大欠を仕り。主君の御箔の内には。しばらく
も居る事をいやがり。歸りいそぎを仕るも。近頃見苦しきものに候。
初心の武士心得のため仍如件。

For instance, on whatever day of the month is your fixed day to go on guard, you must calculate the time it will take you to get there from your house and allow for the length of the daylight, so that you are ready to take over duty just a little before the actual hour. Some silly fellows waste time by having a smoke when they ought to be starting off, or chatting with their wives or children, and so leave their house late and then have to hurry so that they do not have time to greet people they pass in the street. And when they do get to their destination, they are all covered with perspiration and waving their fans even in cold weather, and then have to make up some plausible excuse for being late on account of some urgent business they had to do.

When a samurai must go on guard at his lord's castle he should never be late for any reason of his own. And if one man makes an effort to be a little early and then has to wait a bit for a comrade who is late, he should not squat down and yawn, neither should he hurry away when his time is up as though reluctant to be in his lord's mansions, for these things do not look at all well.

處變

道中の川越舟渡しに於て。大名と大名との出會に。双方の家來口論に及て申つのり。互の方人多く成て。喧嘩に及び候はゞ。其時の様子次第にて。主人と主人の出入と罷成義可有之。もし双方主人の出入と申すに成ては。落着の所計り難く候。然れば。禍は下より起ると心得。主君の御供道中にては。猶以て物を大事にかけ。我身は申すに及ばず。諸傍輩にも氣を付。理不盡の仕形無之様にと。下々へも能々申付る心得肝要に候。

且又江戸において。主君の御供仕りてありき候に。他の大名衆と途中行違ひの時。双方先供の若者共口論を仕出し喧嘩に及ぶ節は。早く氣を付。道具持の手前より主人の御持鎗を受取。御側近く持て罷在。事の成行様子を見合せ。彌鎭りかね。諸士殘らず拔刀の仕合に及ぶ時は。御駕籠の側へ御馬を牽寄せて。早速召させまいらせ。御鎗の鞘を脱して渡し奉り。其身も拔刀に成て働くと覺悟尤に候。

On the Road

When, in the course of crossing a river or taking a ferry on a journey, two daimyos meet and an argument starts between their respective retainers, and their comrades join in so that a general quarrel breaks out, whether the lords themselves will be involved in it or not depends on how the matter is handled. If both of them become involved, it may be difficult to settle it. Remember that trouble arises from below, so when you travel with your lord take good care to look after not only yourself but your comrades too, and solemnly command everybody down to the lowest servant to make sure that nothing unreasonable occurs during your journey.

If you are escorting your lord on foot in Edo and meet another daimyo on the road, if the young samurai in front exchange words and come to blows you must at once rush to get your master's spears from the spear-bearer and stand by him and see how things develop. And if it proves impossible to keep the peace and all the retainers draw their blades and make ready to enter the fray, you must at once bring your lord's horse up to the side of his palanquin and help him to mount, and then unsheathe his spear and hand it to him, all the while being ready to draw your sword and hold your own.

拠又主君御振舞などの御供して参り候節。御座中に於て。不慮の
義出來致し。御座敷の體。騒動と見及び候に於ては。刀を手に持
玄關へ上り。取次の者に出會。某義は誰が家來何某と申ものにて
候。何とやらん御座敷の躰。物騒がしく相聞え候に付。主人の義を
無心許存じ。是迄罷上り候旨可申。取次の者の返答には。させる
義にては無之候得共。御氣遣の段は御尤に候。其許の御主人様
の御事は。御別條無御座候間。少しも御氣遣無之様にと。御傍輩
中へも御演説被成候へなどゝ可申候。然らば先以大慶仕候。左候
はゞ。主人を御呼出。拙者へ御逢せ給り候様にと申斷り。主君へ
御目に掛退出尤に候。初心の武士心得のため仍如件。

And when you accompany your lord to an entertainment, if anything unruly or improper happens while he is there and you detect a disturbance in the chamber, go to the porch, sword in hand, and announce to the attendants, "I am So-and-so, a retainer of Lord So-and-so, and because things seem a bit uproarious within, I feel somewhat anxious about my lord and so I have come to his assistance." Then maybe the attendants will reply, "We don't think it's serious, though it is natural for you to be worried. But since your lord is in no danger, you can just relax and set your mind at ease." You can report this back to your comrades, who will be delighted to hear it. Then you should ask the attendant to find out whether your lord will receive you, and after you have seen him take your leave at once.

述懐

奉公仕る武士。何事にてもあれ。主君の御爲に對し。一廉ある奉公を仕り。我が心にも。天晴一奉公をば勤めたりと存じ。人も感じ譽るといへ共。主君の御心には。左程の義とも思召入られざるにや。又は御心底には感じ思召といへ共。何ぞ外に相障る事も有之やらん。異なる御恩賞もなく。功勞空しく埋るゝに付。心底に不足を挾さみ。御情なき事と述懐たらだらにて。身に染ぬ奉公を致す者は。兎角に及ばず。心得違の事に候。

戰國の武士の一生の間。幾度といふ事なく軍に立。主君大將の御爲に身命を抛ち。手柄高名を極めたる前に於ては。中々口のきかるゝ義にては無之候。子細は。何を申しても治國の奉公と申すは。疊の上を這廻り。互ひに手の甲をさすり。舌先三寸の勝負を爭ふのみの善惡にて。身命をかけそくの働とては。先づは無之事に候。尤忠義の志に於ては。戰國にても治國にても。替る事は無之。勿論奉公する武士の役義に候。それを奇特と有て御賞美可被成も。被成間敷も。其段は主君の御心次第にて。自分は自分の役義を務るとさへ覺悟致し候得ば。事相濟。何にても不足述懐と申義無之道理に候。初心の武士心得のため仍如件。

Showing One's Feelings

A samurai retainer who has performed some special service for his lord and considers it something extraordinary, while others may think so too and praise him, should understand that the matter may not look the same to the lord himself. Even if he does feel moved inwardly, something else about it may offend him. And so if the retainer garners no reward and thinks his merit has been overlooked, he may be dissatisfied and show what he feels by complaining constantly about his lord's ingratitude. This, it hardly needs to be said, is the error of one who does not appreciate the meaning of service.

The samurai of the civil war period went into the field for battle innumerable times over the course of their service, risking their lives freely for their lords and commanders. Still they did not talk about their own merit or their brave deeds. By comparison, peacetime service means simply shuffling around on the mats, rubbing the backs of the hands, and fighting only verbal battles with three inches of tongue, for better or worse. It certainly is nothing like risking one's life in war. But whether in peace or war it is the duty of samurai to serve in that same spirit of loyalty. Whether what they do is anything special or praiseworthy is for their lord to judge. It is enough that they resolve to do their duty properly, and they are not called on to express any feelings of discontent.

忠死

奉公を勤る武士。主君の御恩情を深厚に罷蒙り。其御恩の報じ奉り様無之。せめては殉死なり共仕り度存ずるといへ共。公義の御法度なれば。其義も不相叶。さればとて畳の上に於て。人並の奉公を務めて。一生を過すと申すは。心外の至りなり。あはれ何事にてもあれ。諸傍輩の腕先に叶ひがたき。奉公所もあれかし。身命を抛ち。是非仕り上べき物をと。心底に思ひ定めたる者有之候はゞ。殉死には百双倍も優り。主君の御爲は申すに及ばず。家中大小の諸奉公人までの援ひともなり。忠義勇の三つを兼備へて。末世の武士の手本共可罷成一品有之候。

其子細を申すに。大身の家には。必久しき怨霊有之物に候。其怨霊の崇をなすに其品二つ有之。一つには。其家代々の家老年寄の中に。忠義勇兼備り。後々は必定主君の御用に相立。家中末々の爲にも可罷成とて。諸人の譽事に預る若手の武士。不慮の怪我を致して相果るも。又時の流行煩などにて若死を致し。主人に事を欠せ申候。武田信玄の士大將。甘利左衛門が馬より落て若死を致したるを。是則武田の家の久しき怨霊なりと。高阪彈正が悔みし類ひに候。二つには。其家の家老年寄。其外近習の士の中に於て。主君の御氣に入。外には並ぶ者もなく。出頭致す士の心に入かはり。主人の心を惑はし。非義非道の行ひをさせ申す類ひに候。

Loyal Unto Death

A samurai in service is under a great debt to his lord. He may think that he can hardly repay it except by committing *junshi* and following him in death. But ritual suicide is not permitted by law, and to perform the ordinary service at home on the mats is far from desirable. What then is left? A man may wish for an opportunity to do something more outstanding than his comrades, to throw away his life and accomplish something, and if he resolutely makes up his mind to do something of this kind it is a hundred times preferable to performing *junshi*. For so he may become the savior, not only of his lord, but of all his fellow retainers both small and great, and thus become a great man who will be remembered to the end of time as a model samurai possessing the three qualities of Loyalty, Faith, and Valor.

Now there is always an evil spirit that haunts the family of a person of rank. The way he curses that family is, in the first place, by causing the death by accident or epidemic disease of some young samurai among the hereditary councilors or elders who has the three virtues of a warrior and who promises to be of great value in the future as a support to his lord, as well as a benefit to all the clan, and whose loss is therefore a severe blow. Thus when Amari Saemon, commander of the samurai to Takeda Shingen, fell from his horse and was killed while still young, that was the doing of the vicious spirit of Takasaki Danjo, who had long haunted that house. In the second place, this evil spirit will enter the body of one of the councilors or elders or samurai in attendance whom the lord most trusts and favors so that he may delude the lord's mind and seduce him into the ways of injustice and immorality.

扱右出頭の士主君の心を惑はし候に。大躰六つの品有之候。

一つには。主君の御耳目を塞ぐ分別を仕り。己が同役同職たり共。外々の者は存寄を申事ならず。たとひ申ても。御用ひ不被成様に致し成し。其家の大事小事共に。己一人して申承るに付。主君には此者なくてはと。思召様に仕なすものに候。

二つには。近習徘徊の士の中に。少しは志も有之。主君の御爲にも可罷成と見ゆるものをば。左右に事を寄て。役儀を改め。御側を遠ざけ。己が由緒有もの。又は手前へ心を寄せ。追従軽薄を致し。我が申付る義を。いやと言ぬ者のみ取持て。近習の役人となし置。己が身の奢り。私を致す義を。主君の御耳へ入ぬ様にと分別仕り候。

Now, in thus leading his lord astray this samurai may do so in six different ways.

First, he may prevent him from seeing or hearing anything and fix it so that the others in attendance cannot state their views, or, even if they can, that they are not adopted. He can generally manage things in such a way that his master thinks of him alone as indispensable and commits everything to his keeping.

Second, if he notices that any of the samurai around the household seem promising and likely to be useful to their lord, he will so work things that he is transferred somewhere else and kept away from his master. He will make sure that connections of his own, or men who agree with him and are subservient and respectful to him and never oppose him, are the only ones permitted to come near the lord. Thus he prevents his master from knowing anything about the extravagant and domineering way he lives.

三つには。主君の御心を蕩かし。且は内縁の爲にもと存ずるを以
て。兎角御子孫御相續に增たる義無御座と申立。何者の娘子供と
いふ吟味もなく。美目貌さへよくはと申して。女中集を致し。其外琴
ひき三線ひき。舞子踊子など申す類ひの者迄をも拘へ集め。時折
節の氣延氣晴しは。無て叶ひ不申と誘めまゐらするに付。元來不
足に生れ付被成たる主君の義は申に及ばず。才智發明なる御生
れ付にても。色の道には迷ひ易きを以て。頓て御分別相違あられ。
其戲れを面白きと思召付ては止事なく。次第に物ごく成り。後々は
晝夜の界もなく。亂舞の跡は必酒宴と申様に成行。ひたすら奥ば
いりのみ被成に付。表向家中の用事。領内の仕置をば。悉皆餘所
事の様に思召。御心に染ず外の家老年寄などの。御前へ罷出度と
申すをばいやがり被成。萬づの義を。件の壹人を以て。埒を明け
被成に付。其者の威勢は日々に盛になり外の家老年寄は。有無の
様子に成り。肩身を窄めて閉口仕り。萬端に付。宜しからぬ家風と
成行候。

四つには。右の様子なれば。人の知らぬ内證にて費の物入多く。
償ひの致し方無之に付ては。前代の仕置に背きたる。新法の簡略
を仕出し。爰にせこを入。彼所にさつとを込め。家中へ渡すべき物
をも渡さず。下の諸人大きに痛み苦しみ。迷惑仕る勘辨は毛頭無
之。主君の御事は。被成度まゝの費侈りを被成候故。家中大小の
諸奉公人。口に出してこそ言ね。心には各不足を抱き。誰壹人身に
染て。忠義を勵む者も無之ものに候。

Third, he may persuade his lord to take a secondary consort, using the argument that he lacks sufficient descendants to ensure the succession of his family name and estates. Then he can procure women for this purpose without looking into their family background, as long as they are good to look at. And he can gather dancers and players on the *biwa* and *samisen* and assure his lord that they are essential to divert him and dispel his boredom. And even a lord who is by nature clever and energetic is apt to be led astray by feminine charms, much more than one who is born lacking in these qualities. And then his good judgment will leave him and he will think only of pleasure, becoming more and more addicted to it, so that eventually he will be entirely given up to dancing and merrymaking, inevitably followed by drinking parties at all times of the day and night. In that way he will come to spend all his time in the ladies' apartments without a thought for his official and administrative business, and hating even the idea of meeting with his councilors to talk about these subjects. Therefore, everything remains in the hands of the one evil councilor, and day by day his power grows, while all the others become invisible presences with lips shut tight and no courage to speak up, and thus the entire household goes from bad to worse.

In the fourth place, it follows that under these circumstances, since everything is kept secret, expenses mount and income has to be augmented, so that the old regulations are tossed aside and new ones enacted, and a spy is put in here and someone scolded there and allowances are greatly trimmed. In this manner the lower ranks will find themselves in reduced circumstances and no one will care in the least about it, and all so that their lord may have plenty and live in the lap of luxury. So that, though they dare not speak of it publicly, the greatest discontent runs rampant among all the retainers, and before long none remains who is single-heartedly loyal to his lord.

五つには。大名たるもの。弓矢の道を不沙汰可被成様とては無之
候得共。件の壹人武道不心懸にて。かゝる芽出度静謐の御代に
は。武備の吟味穿鑿には不可及と申すに付。元來不嗜なる家中の
諸人。それを好事に致して。武藝を務めず。武具兵具の用意も致さ
ず。何事も只當座の間さへ合ばよきぞと申す家風なれば。其御先
祖に。世に聞えある名將のおはしましたる家柄の様には少しも無
之。只明日にも事の變有之に於ては。大きに狼狽騒たるばかりに
て。事の埒は一つも明兼可申と。覺束なき次第に候。

六つには。主君の御事。遊興酒色に長じ被成に付。次第に御氣隨
もつのり。剩へ病身にまで御成候へば。家中の諸士氣を屈し。心の
まめしげなく。一日暮しの様子なれば。世間の取沙汰。上の思召不
可然。畢竟のつまり。主君の御身上にも相障り可申か。然れば大き
なる物怪也。其根取を仕る件の壹人は。當家の悪魔。主君の怨敵
と申て。家中こぞりて是を惡み候へ共。十人が九人迄も。其者の惡
事を申立。公事沙汰に取結び。手を汚さず。舌先の勝負にして。本
意を遂べきといふ分別相談の外無之。左候ては。中々内證にて埒
明ず。主君の御一門方の御取扱と成り。それより事重く成行。畢竟
は公義の御沙汰共不罷成しては不叶候。

In the fifth place, though a daimyo is one who should never be anything but experienced in the Way of the Warrior, since the evil councilor is not likely to care anything about it in an age of peace and quiet such as this, there will be no interest at all in military matters and no inspections of the armed forces. And everyone in the household will be rather pleased to fall in with this attitude, and none will bother to think about military duties or make proper provisions for weapons and supplies, and instead will be perfectly content to let things alone and just make do for now. So nobody would think, seeing the current condition of the house, that their ancestors had been warriors of great renown. And if some crisis should erupt and catch them by surprise, there would be nothing but anxious running about and confusion and nobody would know what to do.

In the sixth place, when the lord is thus addicted to pleasure, drink, and consorting with loose women, he will grow more and more wayward until his health becomes affected. All his retainers will lose their morale and be lacking in sincerity, merely living from one day to the next and without any guidance from above. Eventually something may happen to the lord through the influence of this evil spirit. This man who is at the bottom of it all, this vengeful enemy of his master and evil genius of his house, will surely be cursed by all the clan. But even then there will be no cure for it, unless some nine or ten of them plot to accuse him and bring him to judgment by a war of argument without even getting their hands dirty. In that case the affair cannot be cleared up without going public with it, and the lord and his house will be brought up for examination, and then matters may become more serious and end in sentence being passed on them by the shogun's government.

昔が今に至るまで。大名方の家の仕置を被成兼。公義の御厄介と
成り。其事の濟たる上に於て。主人の身上の相立たる例とては無
之。角を直すとて牛を殺し。鼠を狩とて社を燒喩の如く。主人の御
身上は潰れ。家中大小の諸奉公人は。皆々流浪の身と成果申候。
斯る時。前に申す當家の惡魔。主君の怨敵たる。件の大惡人を執
て押へ。胴腹を刎り候とも。又は元首を刎捨候共。心の儘に仕澄し
て堵を明け。我が身は即座に切腹を遂げ相果尤に候。

然る時は。何の出入公事沙汰と申義も無之。主君の御身上に相障
る義も無之。家中の諸人も安堵致し。國家安泰に候。爰を以て殉
死には百双倍も優り忠義勇の三つに相叶ひ。末代の武士の手本
共可罷成一品とは申にて候。初心の武士心得のため仍如件。

In all ages, when a daimyo has been unable to manage his affairs and has been disciplined by the government, the result has been that his house has come to an end. As the proverb has it, "When you straighten the horn you kill the ox, and when you hunt the rats you burn the shrine." So when the lord's house is ruined, his retainers are dismissed and lose their livelihood. Therefore it is best to seize this great rascal of a councilor who is the evil spirit of the house and either stab him through the heart or cut off his head, whichever you prefer, and so put an end to him and his corrupt practices. And then right away you must commit *seppuku* yourself.

Thus there will be no open criminal case or lawsuit or sentence and your lord's person will not be dishonored, so that the entire clan will continue to live in security and there will be no open trouble in the empire. One who acts thus is a model samurai who does a deed a hundred times better than *junshi,* for he possesses the three qualities of Loyalty and Faith and Valor and will hand down a glorious name to generations to come.

文雅

武士道は。剛強の意地あるを第一と仕るは。勿論の義に候得共。
片向に強き計りにては。何とやらん農人上りの武士を見る様にて
不可然候。學問は勿論。其餘暇には。歌學。茶の湯など。少しづゝ
は相心得罷在度事にて候。先學問無之候ては。古今の道理を辨
へ可申様無之に付。其身何ほど世智賢くさし當り利發にても。事
に臨み差支多きものに候。異國本朝の義を粗々覺悟いたし。時と
所と位との三つをよく考へ合せて。其宜きに隨ひ。事を取計らひ候
へば。物に致し毀ひと申義は。左のみ無之ものに候。爰を以て學問
は勿論とは申にて候。但し心得惡しく候へば。大方は我慢になり。
無學文盲なる者をば。目八分に見こなし。其上異國贔負をいたし。
何もかも唐流を善と心得。たとひ道理は善にもせよ。本朝の今時に
は。用ひ難きといふ勘辨もなく。片情を張りて物を申す様なるは。散
々の事に候。爰を分別致して學問尤に候。

Matters Literary and Aesthetic

Though Bushido naturally implies, first of all, the qualities of strength and forcefulness, to have only this one side developed is to be nothing but an unsophisticated samurai of no great importance. So a samurai ought to be literate, and, if he has time, should take up verse-making or Teaism, to a certain extent. For if he does not study he will not be able to understand the reasons of things, either past or present. And however worldly-wise or sagacious he may be, he will find himself greatly handicapped at times for lack of learning. If you have a general understanding of the affairs of your own country and of foreign lands and carefully consider the three principles of Time and Place and Rank, and follow the best course, you are not likely to make many mistakes as you go through life. And that is why I assume that a samurai should be studious. But if he makes bad use of his knowledge and grows opinionated and looks down on the illiterate as being a bit dumb, and if he becomes a worshiper of all things foreign and thinks nothing any good if it is not Chinese, and is so prejudiced that he cannot see that a thing may be unsuitable for Japan at the present time, even though it may be good in theory, then I say that his learning is too much of a good thing. With this in mind, he should study.

次に歌學の義は。和朝の風俗にして。古今の名將勇士の中に。歌道の達人も有之候。然れば小身の武士たり共。歌道に立入。折にふれたる腰折の一首も。綴り候程にはあり度事に候。然れ共萬事を抛ち。歌學のみを專らと致す時は。いつとなく心も貌もなま和らかに。公家侍を見る様になりて。武士の風俗を取失ふものにて候。就中今時世にもてはやし候俳諧など。數寄過候へば。隔意がましき傍輩の出會に於ても。やゝもすれば。輕口出來口秀句などを申し。當分は一座の興にも成り候へ共。武士たる者は愼むべき事に候。

倡茶の湯の義も。京都將軍家の時代より。專ら武家の玩びとなり候へば。たとひ我が手前にてこそ數寄を致さずとも。人の許へ招れ。或は貴人高位の御相伴などにも。參る間敷に非ず。左様の刻。路次入數寄屋入の次第。所々の飾り置合せの見様。或は料理の給様。茶の飲様にも。種々の心得有之由なれば。茶道方に於て指南を受。少しは學び置可然候。

其上數寄屋の義は。世間の富貴榮耀を離れ。幽居閑栖の境界を樂しむを以て。いか程繁榮の地。又は官家の内たり共。庭には山林溪谷の風景を寫し。竹の椽。皮付の柱。苅ふける軒端。下地窓。篠すだれ。猿戸しをり戸等の。佗たる粧ひを宗と仕り。其外茶具會席の具に至るまで。美麗を好まず。專ら塵世を厭ひ避けて。偏へに清閑自然の象を樂しむを以て。本意と仕り候へば。武士道の氣味を甘なふ爲の。助け共可罷成様にも被存候。

Verse-making is a custom of our country, and great soldiers in all ages have been distinguished in it, so even a humble retainer would do well to go in for it and try his hand at a clumsy verse on occasion. But anyone who gets entirely absorbed in it and neglects his ordinary duties will become soft in mind and body and lose all martial qualities and look like nothing but a courtier-samurai. Particularly if you get too fond of these short *haikai* verses that are now so fashionable, you may easily start acting slick-tongued and witty and smart even in the company of grave and reserved colleagues, and though this may be amusing in society at the present time it is an attitude samurai ought to avoid.

Then, as for *cha-no-yu,* from the days of the Kyoto shoguns this tea ceremony has been very much the diversion of the military class. Even though you are not yourself a great enthusiast yet, you are likely to be invited to take part in it and be a fellow-guest with people of high degree, so you ought to know at least how to enter the tea-room and its precincts properly, how to view table arrangements and perform ceremonies intelligently, and how to eat the meal and drink the tea correctly. To obtain this knowledge of the rules of the procedure it is advisable to take some lessons from a tea-master.

Again, the tea-room is a place very profitable for the enjoyment of retirement and tranquility far removed from boastful display and luxury, so that even in the grounds of the wealthy and of officials you find these reed-thatched huts with their pillars of natural wood and their rafters of bamboo set in what seems to be a solitary mountain valley with their bare simplicity of plain lattice window, bamboo blind, and rustic wicket gate and entrance. And the tea vessels and other utensils are equally without any gaudy ornament, but are of clean and restrained form that entirely avoids the impurities of everyday life. If cultivated, this spirit is, I think, of great assistance in sweetening the Way of the Warrior.

然ればたとひ茶たつる所をしつらひ候共。新筆の掛物。今燒の茶
入茶碗。土罐子等の輕き茶具を用ひて。侘茶の湯を樂むほどの義
は。惡しきにあらず候。然れ共萬事輕きが重くはなり易く。程次く奢
が付て。人の所持致す芦屋の釜を見ては。手前の土釜がいやにな
り。それにつれて一切の茶具共に。次第に好ものを欲しくなり。い
つしか掘出しの心懸となり。目利を仕習ひ。價少なにて。宜しき道
具を取出す分別を仕り。或は人の許に。何ぞしほらしき物もあれ
ば。平所望を仕り。又は道具替などに致すとても。我が方へ徳を取
分別を專一と仕り。悉皆とり賣中買など申す。町人の意地に均しき
樣子にて。武士道の正義を取失ひ。大きに惡しき人柄と罷成候。
左樣の數寄者とならむよりは。一向茶道不案内にて。濃茶とやらん
はいか樣に飲といふを。存ぜぬ程の不調法にても。それは武士道
の抑へには成らぬ事に候。初心の武士心得のため仍如件。

おろかなる筆のすさみも直かれと
　　　子をおもふ親のかたみとは見よ

So it is no bad thing for anyone to make a place for *cha-no-yu* if he has only pictures by present-day artists and tea utensils by modern potters and an earthenware tea-kettle so that it is all inexpensive and in accordance with the austere style of Teaism. But in all things the simple is apt to become complicated, and luxury may show itself. For instance, if when you see someone else's Ashiya ironwork kettle you feel disgusted with your own earthenware one, you will soon come to want all your utensils to be things of value. Then you will cultivate an eye for a bargain and go in for the finer things, so that you can pick up a worthy piece for a small sum. Then, if you see anything very attractive at somebody's house you will plead with him for it or else want to give him something in exchange, with, of course, the intention of getting the best of it yourself. This kind of thing is no better than the nature of a huckster or peddler and degrades the Way of the Warrior to that of the mere shopkeeper. It is a very bad fault, and rather than practice this kind of Teaism, it is better to know nothing about it at all, and to remain ignorant of even how to drink powder tea. For it is preferable to appear a little uncouth than to spoil the quality of Bushido.

Although little more than nonsense written off the top of my head, regard this as similar to a memento from a parent who hopes his children will lead honest and straightforward lives.

Other Books from Ulysses Press

The Art of War
Sun Tzu, translated by Lionel Giles, $12.95
Now in a dual-language edition, the timeless wisdom of Sun Tzu's *The Art of War* offers even greater insight by allowing readers to directly compare the Chinese characters of Sun Tzu with the highly respected English translation of Lionel Giles.

Jesus and Buddha: The Parallel Sayings
Marcus Borg, Editor   Introduction by Jack Kornfield, $14.00
This book traces the life stories and beliefs of Jesus and Buddha, then presents a comprehensive collection of their remarkably similar teachings on facing pages.

The Lost Sutras of Jesus: Unlocking the Ancient Wisdom of the Xian Monks
Edited by Ray Riegert & Thomas Moore, $11.95
Combines the amazing story and remarkable text of the Xian monks into a fascinating historical journey and spiritual quest.

To order these books call 800-377-2542 or 510-601-8301, fax 510-601-8307, e-mail ulysses@ulyssespress.com, or write to Ulysses Press, P.O. Box 3440, Berkeley, CA 94703. All retail orders are shipped free of charge. California residents must include sales tax. Allow two to three weeks for delivery.